P9-BXW-961

KAKAPO RESCUE

Saving the World's Strangest Parrot

Houghton Mifflin Books for Children is an imprint of
Houghton Mifflin Harcourt Publishing Company.

www.hmhbooks.com

Book design by YAY! Design
The text of this book is set in Gill Sans.

Library of Congress Cataloging-in-Publication Data is on file.
ISBN 978-0-618-49417-0

Printed in Singapore
TWP 10 9 8 7 6 5 4 3 2 1
4500202650

KAKAPO RESCUE

Saving the World's Strangest Parrot

Text by Sy Montgomery *Photographs by* Nic Bishop

Houghton Mifflin Books for Children
Houghton Mifflin Harcourt
Boston New York 2010

For Mike Meads, who saved the giant weta from extinction, and made me fall in love with New Zealand.
—S.M.

To Deidre, who helped make this book possible, and to all those who work on the front lines to protect species.
—N.B.

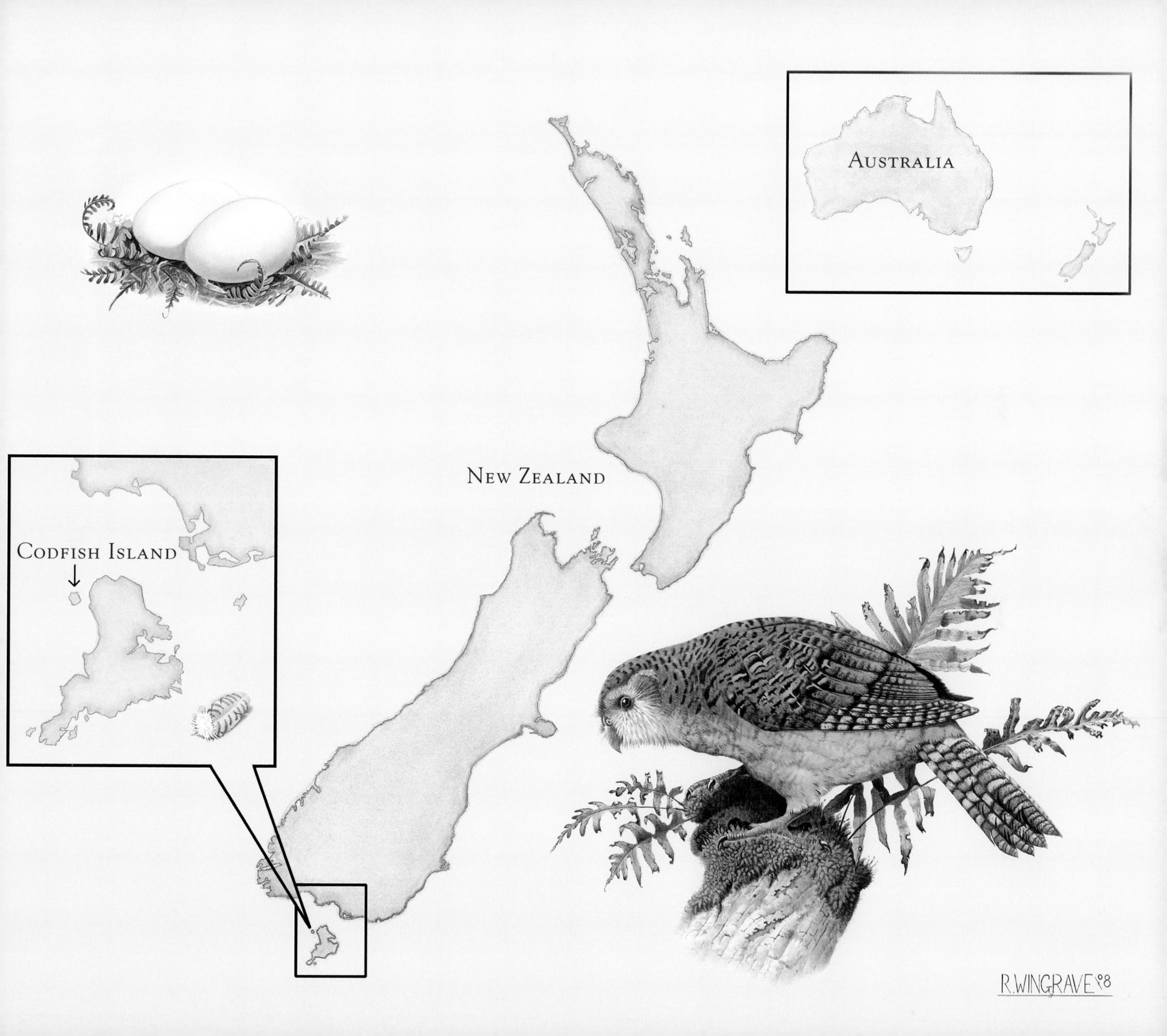
Australia
New Zealand
Codfish Island
R.WINGRAVE '98

Decked in beautiful moss-green feathers, a kakapo explores the forest at night.

CHAPTER 1

THE STRANGEST PARROT IN THE WORLD

It's hours past midnight. You'd think any self-respecting parrot would be asleep. But not Lisa.

No, despite the late hour, this huge, soft, moss-green bird, looking somewhat like a parakeet who has eaten one side of the mushroom in *Alice in Wonderland* and grown into an eight-pound giant, decides this is a great time to waddle out of her nest—a nest that's not in a tree, like a normal parrot's, but *underground*.

Reaching the surface, she begins her nightly explorations of the forest. Does she take off and soar from tree to tree? No—this bird travels only on foot. Even though her wings are healthy, she can't fly. Tonight, she'll thrash noisily through the underbrush in the dark, looking for food. She'll sleep hidden from view during the day.

Is Lisa a winged weirdo? A perverse parrot? No, everything she's doing is perfectly normal—for a kakapo (KAR-ka-poe), that is. Found only in New Zealand, the kakapo is the rarest and heaviest parrot, the only flightless and night-active parrot, and undoubtedly the strangest parrot in the world.

But what happens tonight in a nearby tent is stranger still.

Ding-dong!

Few tents come equipped with doorbells, but this one does. It sounds inside the tent the second that Lisa crosses an infrared beam as she leaves her nest. Scientists set up the contraption to ensure that the two sleepy women in the tent are awakened each time Lisa goes for a walk. The time has come for them to do a very important job. The two volunteers are "nest-minders"—

Volunteer nest-minders Lynnie Gibson and Catherine Tudhope spend each night camping in the forest, where they watch over Lisa's comings and goings on a small video monitor.

sort of like nannies. They're nannies for an extraordinary baby.

As Lisa forages, she leaves behind a single blind, downy chick. Unlike familiar birds such as robins, kakapo moms and dads don't raise their babies together. But Lisa's got plenty of help. Fifty yards from the nest, the two campers wriggle out of their sleeping bags and tug on pants, boots, warm jackets, and hats. Guided by flashlights, they make their way to the nest in the dark. Their mission? To place a warm blanket over the chick, so it won't get chilled while Mama looks for food.

The helpless white baby is precious beyond measure. It is the only kakapo chick in the world right now—one of just eighty-seven kakapo on the planet.

Though they used to be common all over New Zealand, kakapo now live only on two small islands off New Zealand's southern coast. That's why we've come here to windswept Codfish Island, a cliffy, forest-clad five-square-mile speck of land just twenty degrees north of Antarctica. This is the kakapo's only breeding area—the nonbreeders have all been taken to an island called Anchor. The entire human population of Codfish—fourteen of us at the moment—is here working toward the same goal: to help save the kakapo from extinction. And we are hoping that any day now, there will be eighty-eight kakapo, eighty-nine kakapo . . . and maybe even more.

We could not have come at a more exciting moment. Kakapo don't breed every year. They don't even breed every other year. In fact, no one can predict with certainty when they'll breed at all. So much about this strange bird is a mystery.

Few people ever get to see a kakapo. Not even volunteers who come to Codfish year after year. You can hike the island all day long and never see a kakapo—they're all asleep. Volunteer nest-minders often wait for years to get the call that they'll be needed.

The special forest rangers here, known as kakapo protection officers, and the technical support officers—all part of New Zealand's National Kakapo Recovery Team—are very excited. This is shaping up to be the most important season in some of the rangers' entire careers. I have been waiting five years to write the words in this book for you, and photographer Nic Bishop has been waiting just as long to bring you these pictures.

We could not have imagined a stranger or more beautiful place. We're visitors in a topsy-turvy world, where everything seems upside down: though March is spring in North America, in New Zealand, it's autumn. On Codfish Island, birds nest in fall, wild creatures seem tame, parrots don't fly, and night is as busy as day. In the dark, the forest seems magical, full of mosses, ferns, and moonlight, alive with sounds like bells and flutes, pops and buzzes—the voices of birds and bats who travel and sing at night, like mischievous goblins.

But even in this enchanted setting, we're in a race against time. We could be witness to one of the most thrilling conservation success stories in human history—or one of its noblest but most tragic failures.

This March, the future of the species is cradled in two nests, three incubators, and the hearts and hands of the kakapo-loving humans who've come from around the world to help.

After all, we owe it to the bird. For it was our kind that nearly wiped it out in the first place.

KAKAPO Fast Facts

- Weighing up to nine pounds, the kakapo is the world's heaviest parrot. (Because of their long tails, many parrots, such as macaws, are bigger than the kakapo—but none is heavier.)
- The kakapo's flat, yellowish, owl-like face has whiskers like a cat's—to help it get around in the dark.
- First described by scientists in 1895, the kakapo has a Latin name of *Strigops* (owl-face) *habroptilus* (soft-feathered). Why are the feathers so soft? They don't need to be strong and stiff for flying.
- Kakapo don't talk, but they can growl like a dog, boom like a bullfrog, and ching like a cash register.
- The kakapo's feathers smell strongly of honey, a scent produced by harmless bacteria.
- Though kakapo can't fly, they climb high in trees using their massive feet and beaks. To get back down, they jump with wings spread—and drop onto thick layers of forest carpet like a stone.
- Kakapo can live to be at least seventy years old—and likely to more than one hundred.
- The word *kakapo* comes from the words for parrot (*kaka*) and night (*po*) in the Maori language. The plural of *kakapo* is not *kakapos* but *kakapo*; there is no s added in the Maori language for plurals.

Some of the last kakapo to survive on mainland New Zealand were discovered on the almost vertical mountains of Sinbad Gully in Fiordland.

CHAPTER 2

THE EXTINCTION THAT ALMOST HAPPENED

Imagine shaking the trunk of a sapling and finding giant parrots falling to the ground like apples! That's how common kakapo once were in New Zealand. In the late 1800s, if you went camping in New Zealand's bush, these curious giant parrots might waddle from the forest to visit your evening campfire or investigate your tent.

Millions of kakapo once thrived all over New Zealand. Polynesian settlers feasted on them. The birds were so easy to catch that Maori people ate them like chicken and made cloaks from the soft, honey-scented feathers.

The first European naturalists to study kakapo found them irresistibly adorable. "One of the most wonderful, perhaps, of all living birds" was how the curator of the British Museum of London described the species when the first living specimen reached Europe in 1870. He was right: Sweet-smelling, beautiful, big, soft, trusting, and playful, kakapo steal your heart.

Sir George Grey, a nineteenth-century naturalist and scholar, kept one as a pet in 1854. At his house, the parrot tumbled about the floor, playing with toys like a kitten. In calmer moments, it snuggled up to him like a dog. A Mr. G. S. Sale, in 1870, found his pet kakapo exceptionally affectionate: "The highest compliment it can pay you," he wrote, "is to nestle down on your hand, ruffle out its feathers and lower its wings, flapping them alternately, and shaking its head from side to side; it is in a superlative state of enjoyment." A Major Murray received a kakapo as a present from the explorer Captain John Lort Stokes and reported that the parrot loved playing with his children. The bird used to waddle after the kids around the garden, following them wherever they went.

But by 1950, all the kakapo were gone. Or so people thought.

No one was particularly surprised. After all, what chance did this curious, gentle giant stand in a place that had changed so much, so fast?

For eons, New Zealand was ruled by birds. No mammals but seals and bats inhabited any of New Zealand's islands. The kakapo's only predators were other birds—hawks and eagles. But wisely, since the raptors flew by day, the night-loving parrots stayed safe by sleeping hidden in scrub or trees or under grass or logs.

Everything changed when a dangerous, new species—humans—showed up about seven hundred years ago. The first people to settle in New Zealand, the Maori, hunted and ate kakapo. And on their long canoe voyage from Polynesia, the Maori brought two new mammals with them that ate the kakapo, too. Maori dogs easily tracked down the strong-smelling kakapo and killed them; and kiore rats, stowaways in Maori canoes, ate the underground chicks and eggs.

But worst of all for the flightless kakapo was the arrival of Europeans after 1769. These new immigrants didn't only hunt kakapo for food. They did something even more destructive: They began to stock New Zealand's islands with all kinds of animals that didn't belong there. Each new ship was a virtual Noah's Ark filled with a flightless vegetarian bird's worst nightmares.

First came two more species of rats. The big, black, climbing ship rat and the still larger brown Norwegian rat were more intimidating, hungrier, and tougher than the Polynesian kiore. Whalers brought cats aboard their ships hoping they'd eat their stowaway rats; but once ashore, the cats ran wild and instead started eating New Zealand's helpless ground-nesting birds. The kakapo was especially vulnerable because its strong scent made it easy for predators to find.

European settlers next brought pigs, deer, goats, and sheep. Their hooves and appetites ruined fragile soil where the kakapo's favorite plants grew. Wishful hunters brought wild rabbits from Europe. Within forty years, the rabbits ate so much ground cover that dust storms prevailed in drought and mudslides struck in rain. Three species of weasels, including ferrets and stoats, were next imported to kill the rabbits—but like the cats, they preferred the helpless native birds.

By the end of the 1800s, the only kakapo left on New Zealand's main islands were confined to the steep, wild forests of Fiordland on South Island. One man tried to save them by moving hundreds to a small island free of predators. But stoats swam to the island. Within only eight years, the stoats had killed every single kakapo.

By the middle of the 1900s, almost everyone thought the kakapo was extinct. Only a few people still held out hope. In the early 1970s, the New Zealand Wildlife Service decided to give the species a last-ditch chance, mounting a series of expeditions to see if any had survived after all—and if they had, to rescue them from the brink of extinction.

More than sixty different expeditions searched for kakapo over twenty-four years. With the help of muzzled dogs, trackers discovered eighteen kakapo surviving in the remote wilderness

Before people settled in New Zealand, its islands were covered in dense forests, rich with unique birds and other animal life.

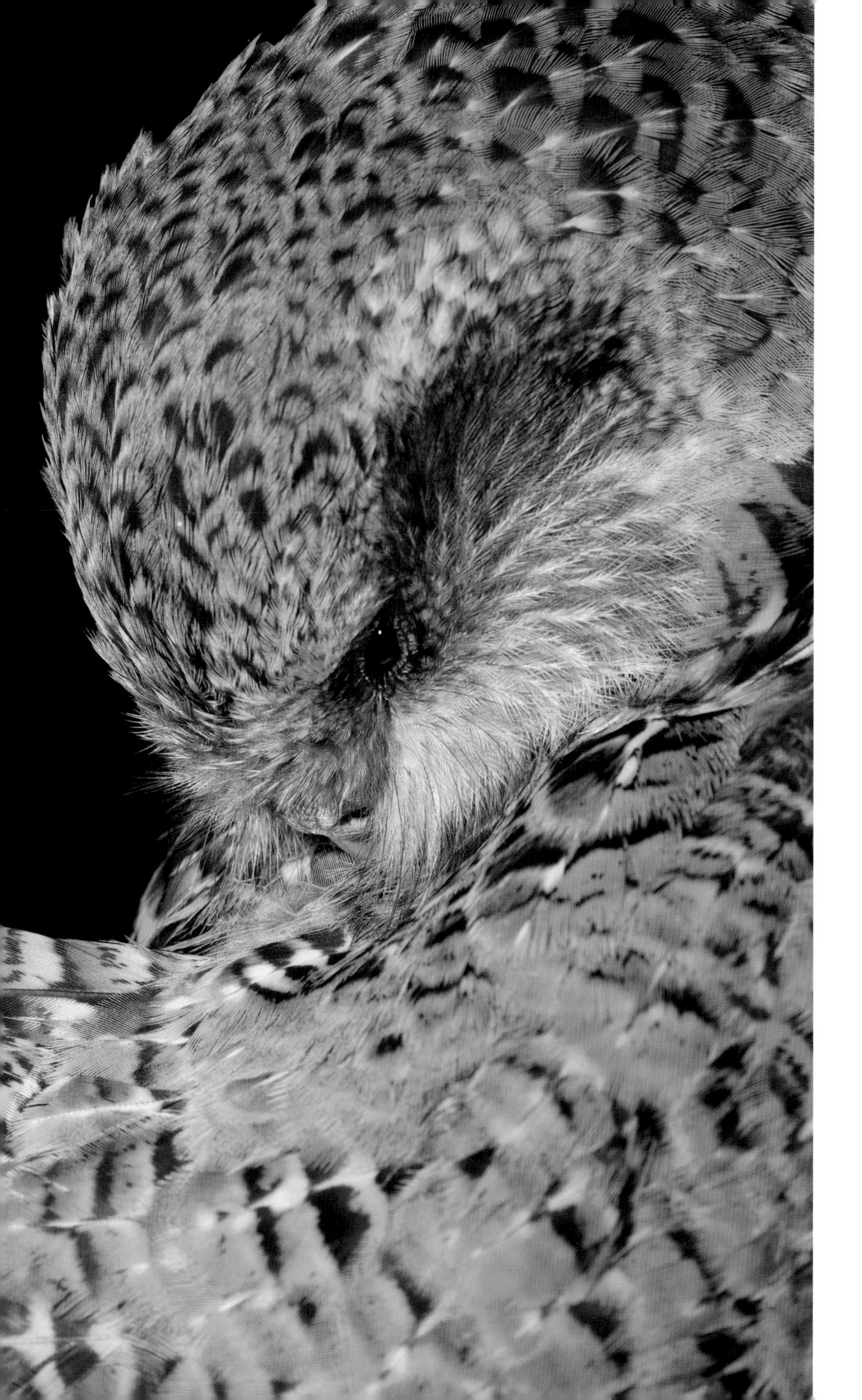

of Fiordland between 1974 and 1977. But then came terrible news: every one of them turned out to be male! The only kakapo known on the planet had no one to breed with. The species was as good as extinct after all.

Unexpectedly, the kakapo got *another* last chance. More expeditions, starting in 1977, uncovered what turned out to be a population of two hundred kakapo on Stewart Island, off the tip of South Island. And this population included the first females seen since the early 1900s.

Here was a rare, last chance for the wildlife service: an opportunity to save the "most wondrous of living birds" from extinction. So began one of the most intensive campaigns in the world to try to save a bird species.

Though Stewart Island was free of weasels and stoats, feral cats were already eating the last kakapo to extinction. Trackers with dogs found, captured, and evacuated every survivor they could find. At last, for the first time in their history, kakapo were airborne: they were moved by plane and by helicopter to safe, predator-free offshore islands. They were joined by five of the males who had been rescued from Fiordland.

Even safe from cats and stoats, the kakapo was still in danger. Not enough kakapo chicks were hatching to replace those dying of old age. Breeding was rare. The chicks didn't always survive. By 1995 there were only fifty-one kakapo on earth. That's when the wildlife service (by then renamed

A kakapo buries its beak into its feathers to preen them.

the Department of Conservation) formed the National Kakapo Recovery Team.

It wasn't enough to just rescue the kakapo from the threats of imported mammals and move them to a safe place. The Department of Conservation had to do more. Scientists, technicians, and volunteers were recruited. They had to try to figure out what inspired the kakapo to breed. They had to learn how to keep the birds healthy. They needed to discover how to get the females to lay more eggs and how to best protect every egg that was laid, every chick who hatched.

The kakapo recovery team made great strides. The kakapo population increased 68 percent in just eight years, to eighty-six birds. But there are still many mysteries to be solved, and the kakapo's future is far from assured.

The pages that follow tell the roller-coaster story of just part of one hatching season, a story of heartbreak and thrills, of hard work and luck, of science and guess-work. And the story's not over, even as I write this book: the best of modern technology, the smartest scientists, the most passionate conservationists, and the most deeply dedicated volunteers are all still struggling to save the kakapo—and to make up for the mistakes of our ancestors.

New Zealand's Splendid Isolation

The forests were tall and ancient. Huge pillar-like kauri trees lived to three thousand years old. Dinosaur-era tree ferns and tall palms with fronds ten feet long towered above an under-story of woodland grasses, soft mosses, lacy ferns, and fragrant orchids. But no deer browsed the bushes. No chipmunks stored nuts below ground. No monkeys swung from treetops, no kangaroos hopped through the grass. There were no lions or tigers, no bears or wolves. Except for a few species of bats, New Zealand's primeval forests hosted no mammals at all. Seals were the only mammals found on its beaches.

Yet this land was full of life. New Zealand was a world ruled by birds.

A thousand miles away from Australia, its nearest neighbor, New Zealand devel-oped a completely different set of creatures than anywhere else on earth. Eighty percent of its trees, ferns, and flowering plants are unique to its islands—so are almost half of its land and sea birds, and nearly all of its reptiles and invertebrates (spineless animals such as bugs, slugs, and spiders). None of its lizards or frogs are found anywhere else.

Thanks to its splendid isolation, New Zealand's bird life has flourished as nowhere else. Many birds took on the roles that mammals do in other forests. The ten-foot-tall, flightless moa—picture monster ostriches with no wings—browsed the trees and bushes like deer. Smaller birds such as wrens and fernbirds scurried through the brush like squirrels and chipmunks. Near-sighted, wingless kiwi probed the earth for tasty worms, much as skunks dig for grubs on suburban American lawns.

For eons upon eons, New Zealand was a peaceful place. With the exception of a giant eagle, *Harpagornis*, and some smaller birds of prey, few predators threatened the other inhabitants. Most birds could relax. That's why so many

Huge carnivorous land snails glide over the forest floor, hunting for worms.

The flightless kiwi's nostrils are at the tip of its long beak so it can sniff for worms and grubs underground.

The giant weta is one of the world's largest insects. It dines on seeds, berries, leaves, and other insects, dead or alive.

Throughout the islands, ancient forest stretched from mountains to sea when the first people arrived in New Zealand.

of them were flightless like the kakapo or had small, weak wings like the fernbird. Some—like the moa and kiwi—lacked wings altogether. With no land-bound predators to harm them, they had no need for flight. Even the insects had remarkably few worries. They didn't need to hide from anteaters or armadillos, skunks or bears. They didn't have to compete for food with moles or voles or mice. Many of New Zealand's invertebrates grew into giants—as big as small mammals. New Zealand today hosts the heaviest insect on earth, the giant weta, a cricketlike creature who can weigh three times more than a mouse, and huge, carnivorous land snails with colorful shells as big as your fist.

But what makes New Zealand's creatures so special also made them uniquely vulnerable to the changes humans would bring to their peaceful islands. New Zealand never suffered the plague of big-game hunters that blasted so much of Africa's wildlife into oblivion. It's been spared the pollution that heavy industry brought to America and Europe. But nonetheless, this clean, green nation has suffered one of the highest extinction rates in the world—mostly due to other animals, who were imported to New Zealand by people who thought they could improve on nature's plan.

Instead, the imports were disastrous. By the time the first European sailors landed in 1769, Polynesians had already killed and eaten all eleven species of giant moa into nothingness. The giant eagle that preyed on the moa had nothing to eat; it went extinct, too. And things got even worse very quickly. Europeans not only rapidly felled forests for farms; they imported livestock, pets, and pests from all over the world. By the end of the 1800s, more than forty of New Zealand's unique bird species had gone extinct.

Today, conservationists are desperately trying to save New Zealand's remaining native species. Half of all New Zealand's native birds are threatened, and fifteen of them—including the kakapo—are critically endangered. But the good news is this: The people of New Zealand want to make amends. Saving birds like the kakapo is a national priority.

The sun rises on remote and rocky Codfish Island, one of the most important island wildlife sanctuaries on earth. To the indigenous Maori people, this island is known as Whenua Hou (New Land).

CHAPTER 3

AN ISLAND A WORLD APART

"The first landing will be fine," Gilly Adam, quarantine logistics manager for Southland, predicts. That's good news for Nic and me and our new friends, a ranger, a filmmaker, and a kakapo team volunteer. We're leaving New Zealand's southernmost city, Invercargill, today to fly to the kakapo's remote offshore island.

But the first landing takes us only halfway there, to Stewart Island. What next? Another flight on a different plane—and that might not be so fine. "The wind comes tumbling off the bay here," Gilly continues, pointing to a map on the wall at the Quarantine Office, "and it's a bit dodgy taking off again."

Dodgy? Well, if Codfish Island were easy to get to, it would probably be overrun with sheep, rats, cats, weasels, and people, instead of the safe haven for the kakapo that it is today.

Wild, windy, and rugged, Codfish is a world apart. No stoats, ferrets, or weasels ever came to the island. No people live here except visiting scientists, rangers, and volunteers. Once there were rats, but to protect the rare, native species, wildlife workers killed them off. There aren't even many foreign weeds here. Most of the plants are New Zealand natives. The Quarantine Office and the kakapo team work hard to keep it that way.

Before leaving the mainland, all visitors to Codfish must wash everything in a special strong soap called Trigene that kills bacteria, viruses, and fungi. We washed our pants and hats, polar fleeces and socks, rain gear and thermal underwear with it—even

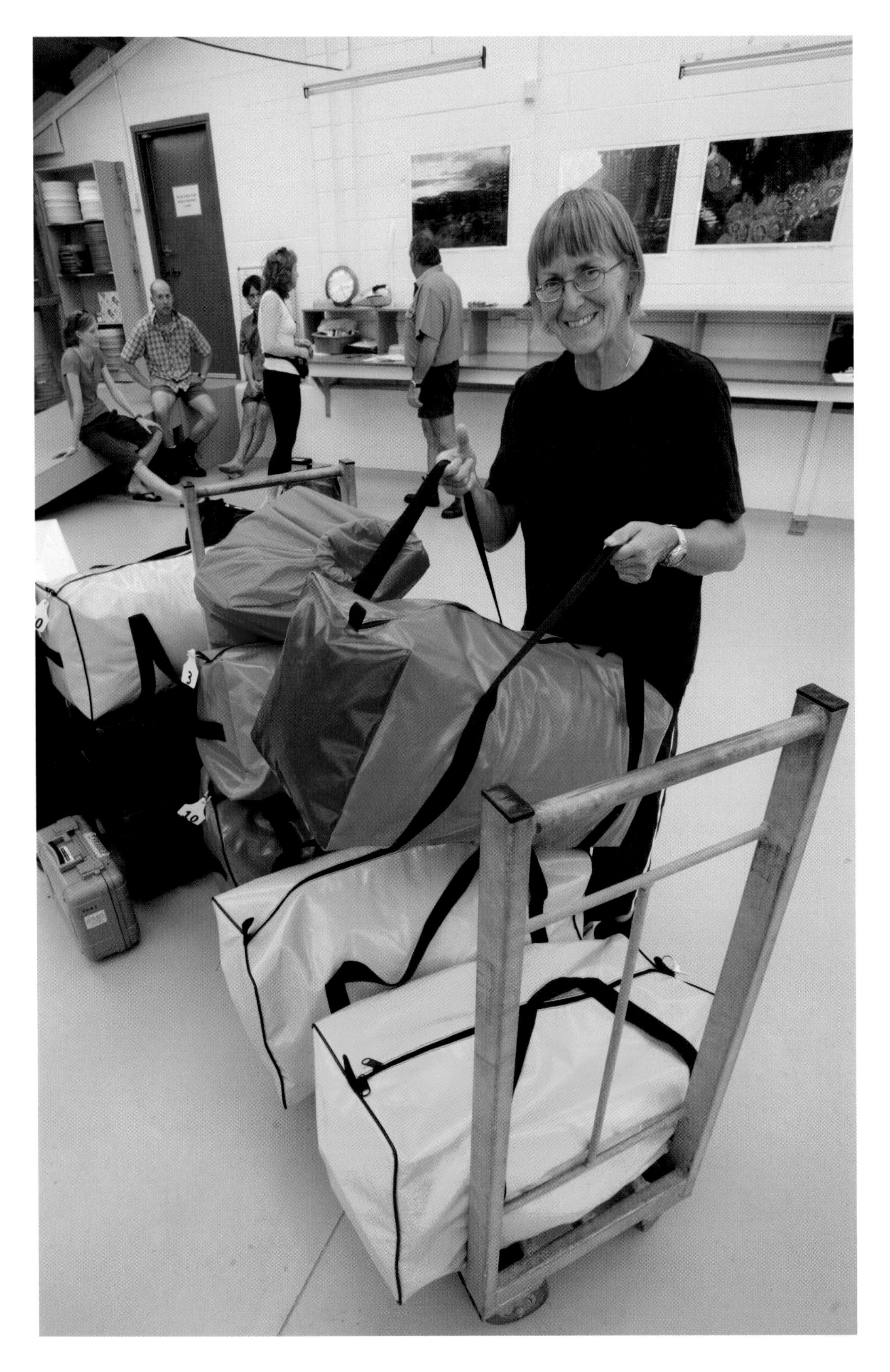

our regular underwear. Nic and I soaked the soles of our boots in it. We sprayed it on our water bottles, on my tape recorder, on Nic's camera equipment, even on the handles of our toothbrushes and the covers of my notebooks. Only the lenses of Nic's cameras were spared—these he wiped with disinfecting alcohol. We couldn't take any chances: The Trigene wash ensures we won't unwittingly spread germs of bird diseases from the mainland or from other countries to the kakapo's island sanctuary.

Before we leave Invercargill, we visit the Quarantine Office. Gilly checks all our gear to make sure it's safe. He turns every pocket inside out, inspects each Velcro closure, examines the treads of our hiking boots and sneakers. Each speck of dirt is scrubbed away; any seed or piece of plant is removed and thrown away. Next we transfer all our gear from our own backpacks and suitcases into special clean bags the Quarantine Office provides. And finally, we change out of the clothes we've worn to the office and into another set we had packed in sealed plastic bags to wear to the island. We leave the old clothes and backpacks behind to pick up later. Only then are we allowed to step into the "Clean" room of the Quarantine Office, and from there proceed to our airplane.

In our eight-seat, propeller-driven plane, we taxi down the grass runway. As the plane climbs, we look down on fields with cows and sheep, homes and trees, all as small as a model

Everything has been checked through quarantine and put into special bags. Volunteer Wendy Bailey loads the bags, ready for our flight to Codfish Island.

We change planes on the remote surf-swept beach of Mason's Bay, Stewart Island.

railroad, as we fly south toward the sea. The white surf looks like feather down. The sunny weather grows gloomy, the sky gray and purple like a bruise, and we see rain in the distance. We're in the latitudes that early sailors dubbed the "Roaring Forties" because of frequent gale-force winds and lashing rain. We're glad we packed warm clothes and rain gear.

Our first stop, Stewart Island, was once one of the kakapo's last strongholds. Most of it is a national park. Its 695 square miles of mountains are draped in forest, and from the plane we see no roads at all. Our pilot makes a test run over our "landing strip"—the sand beach of Mason's Bay—to check for seals and make sure there's enough space to land.

Stewart is rugged and beautiful. Kiwi (possibly as many as twenty thousand) vastly outnumber humans (perhaps four hun-

Sunrise at Sealer's Bay.

dred). But not even this wild place is wild enough to protect the kakapo. That's why we can't linger. We transfer here to a Cessna 185 six-seater. It's raining now, but the wind is relatively calm. We're in luck: Down the beach we go, and bump, bump, bump—we lift off! Heading west, just two miles from Stewart's secluded shores, we'll touch down at the only place on earth where kakapo nest.

Before we've even settled in to the hut where we'll be staying, we can see Codfish Island is an extraordinary place. We land at a spot called Sealer's Bay, where American and European sealers settled with their Maori wives two hundred years ago. Each evening, penguins waddle from the surf across the white sand beach to sleep in forest holes. A short trail leads to where *we'll* sleep: Sealer's Bay Hut, the only permanent building on the island. Under its corrugated tin roof, fourteen of us—volunteers, rangers, technical support officers, filmmaker Scott Mouat, Nic and I—will eat, sleep, and record and process data from the kakapo rescue project.

Miles of trails crisscross this tiny island. The trails have names such as Mudwiggle, Horror, Heinous, Humbug—a good clue they're muddy, treacherous, and not for weekend hikers. No tourists are allowed. No humans live here year-round. The island is about kakapo, not people. The trails have been cut so that researchers and volunteers can get to every kakapo on the island, and ensure the well-being of each one.

Strange objects pepper the trails. Along the sandy path from the beach are baited traps for rats, just in case one manages to stow away on a plane or swim ashore from a fishing boat. There are small white plastic platforms here and there—weighing

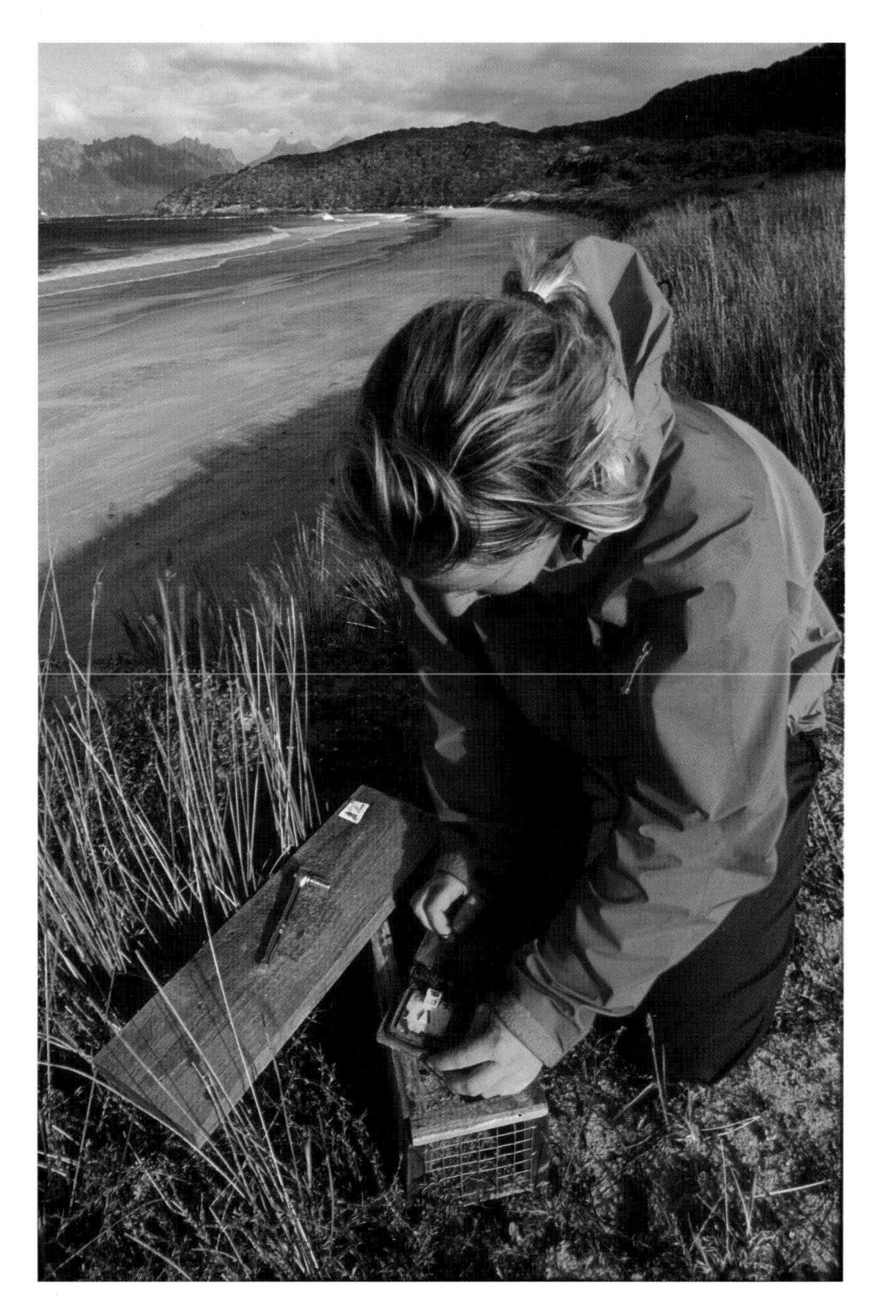

Traps are laid near the coast to catch any rats that manage to swim ashore from passing boats.

Kakapo are tracked by telemetry. Beyond, cool blue ocean stretches south all the way to Antarctica.

stations for kakapo—and small bins with hinged lids—hoppers for the kakapo's supplemental feed. There are low, mysterious-looking black waterproof boxes called snarks. They're well named, after a Lewis Carroll story, "The Hunting of the Snark," about a bird that was impossible to find. And so would be the kakapo, without this equipment: the snarks come with radio receivers to record each kakapo who passes by.

Each bird is outfitted with a backpack that transmits a radio frequency that rangers can track with hand-held telemetry as well as the snarks. Every kakapo here has a name, a history, and a well-mapped territory. Each also has its own feeding station—some birds even have two or three!

Monitoring intensifies as the birds approach the breeding season—if there is one. Sometimes years pass with no breeding at all. Then suddenly, it's like a soap opera; the rangers try to keep up with who mates with whom. Of the thirty-eight adult females on the planet as the New Zealand autumn began, only five of them mated this year. Ten eggs were laid. They look like small chicken eggs. (But you wouldn't want to eat these for breakfast!) Each egg comes into the world with a pedigree, and each carries with it the hopes of wildlife lovers from around the world.

Too often, those hopes are dashed.

This year, Lisa was the first kakapo to lay. The egg died.

Apirima, a first-year nester, laid two eggs. One of them cracked. Unknowingly, while her breast feathers were sticky with the contents of her cracked egg, Apirima dragged the surviving egg outside the nest as she left on her nightly search for food. The egg sat in the cold rain for hours before rangers discovered its plight and rescued it. Now the egg sits cradled in an incubator, in a temporary building just outside the hut.

Apirima's egg is not alone. Sue's and Rakiura's eggs are in an incubator, too. Sue's first egg was removed from the nest in hopes it would encourage her to lay a second one. Farmers sometimes do this with chickens. But instead, Sue abandoned the nest.

Rakiura laid two eggs. But like Apirima, this six-year-old was a young first-time mom. The kakapo team didn't want to take chances with her precious eggs after the disaster with Aparima's. They took her eggs from the nest to hatch them in an incubator.

Cyndy laid three eggs but is only sitting on two. One was removed for artificial incubation after she stayed off the nest one night for three hours.

The other active nest is Lisa's. Though her first egg died, she laid another last month. Nic and I learned it had hatched the day we arrived in New Zealand.

Each kakapo is like a *Mona Lisa*, a Taj Mahal, a Hope Diamond. Each is a treasure of unsurpassed rarity and value. But unlike a painting, a building, or a gem, each kakapo is a living treasure, a treasure that loves its own life. And each kakapo has the potential of no mere object: the power to help restore its kind—with a lot of aid from its human friends.

Kakapo are not the only flightless birds on Codfish. The island is also a refuge for a flightless duck called the Campbell Island teal, which feeds along the coast.

Ancient totara trees and filmy Dracophyllum *bushes grow over a plush carpet of mosses and ferns.*

CHAPTER 4

SECRETS OF THE NEST

"Codfish Base from Lisa's nest." Like an astronaut calling Mission Control from space, nest-minder Catherine Tudhope, a fifty-eight-year-old volunteer from New Zealand's capital city of Wellington, radios the hut to check in. "We've arrived here safely," she reports.

When it's not raining, the forty-five-minute hike up to Lisa's nest from the hut is relatively easy, even with all the gear we have to carry. But even on mild evenings like this one, when hiking warms us up enough to take off our jackets, we know storms—shrieking gale-force winds and lashing, freezing rain—can come suddenly. No one leaves the hut for the trails without warm clothes, rain gear, water, and food.

The trail to Lisa's nest is lined with ferns, orchids, and ancient trees called podocarps that have leathery or needle-like leaves that resemble pine or rosemary. Among them are rimu, whose pinhead-size red fruits are the kakapo's favorite food. Now it's dusk, and as twilight comes on, the dimming light seems to shimmer with the twinkling calls of kakariki parakeets, and the "salt PEA-nuts!" cries of the kaka—a dark-feathered parrot who, unlike the kakapo, can fly.

It's a windswept wilderness, and Catherine and her nest-minding partner, Lynnie Gibson, a forty-eight-year-old mother of four, will sleep the night in a tent. Still, what's the first thing they do as they reach their home for the night?

Check the TV for their favorite soap opera. That's right—

Inside the tent, Lynnie watches over Lisa the kakapo by video.

but there's only one show on this TV, and it's playing what's going on in Lisa's nest, live.

"Lisa's on the nest," Catherine radios Codfish Base. Thanks to a video camera installed in the nest and hooked up to a monitor, the nest-minders can keep a watchful eye on Lisa and her chick. Later, they can review the recording for important clues to kakapo nesting behavior.

"Glad you made it so quickly," ranger Becky Wilson, thirty-three, answers from the hut. "We're sending up Jeff, Jo, and Tristan to join you. Talk with you later."

As we wait for the three rangers to join us, Catherine and Lynnie check the telemetry equipment. Each kakapo has its own channel. Lynnie unfolds her antenna and discovers Lisa's channel is coming in on her receiver loud and clear. Once Lisa leaves the nest and we can no longer see her on the TV monitor, the telemetry will help us keep track of her so we'll know when she's coming back.

By the time the three rangers join us near half past eight, we've been watching Kakapo TV for hours. Lisa has changed position, and now we have a great view of the baby: still egg-shaped, it's blind, helpless, and covered in white down. "It's *so* cute!" exclaims Lynnie.

Around us, the night is coming alive. Short-tailed bats chirp from their singing posts in hollow trees, from which the males call to females. A morepork, New Zealand's only species of owl, calls out its name: "More pork! More pork!"

At 8:29, Lisa dashes off screen. "She's off!" cries Lynnie. A second later, the doorbell chimes in the tent. Lisa has left the nest for the first meal of the night.

Lynnie swings the telemetry antenna to catch Lisa's signal. The parrot's heading straight for the hopper of food that

Like the kakapo, the short-tailed bat is bizarre and rare. Although it can fly, it spends lots of time feeding on the ground. It folds its wings and uses its wrists to scamper along and burrow into the leaf litter like a shrew or a vole in search of insects. This bat has partly given up flight, like many of New Zealand's birds.

volunteers left for her earlier. Quickly, the way lit by flashlight, we head for the nest.

Removing a lid that looks like a manhole cover allows us access to the chick. How did the kakapo team install it? Once the telemetry signals showed that Lisa had chosen a nest site, rangers and tech officers waited till she was out foraging to sneak in. They dug an opening in the nest's ceiling and installed the removable lid.

They were careful to leave the parrot's own entrance to the nest untouched. But surely these curious, intelligent birds noticed something changed!

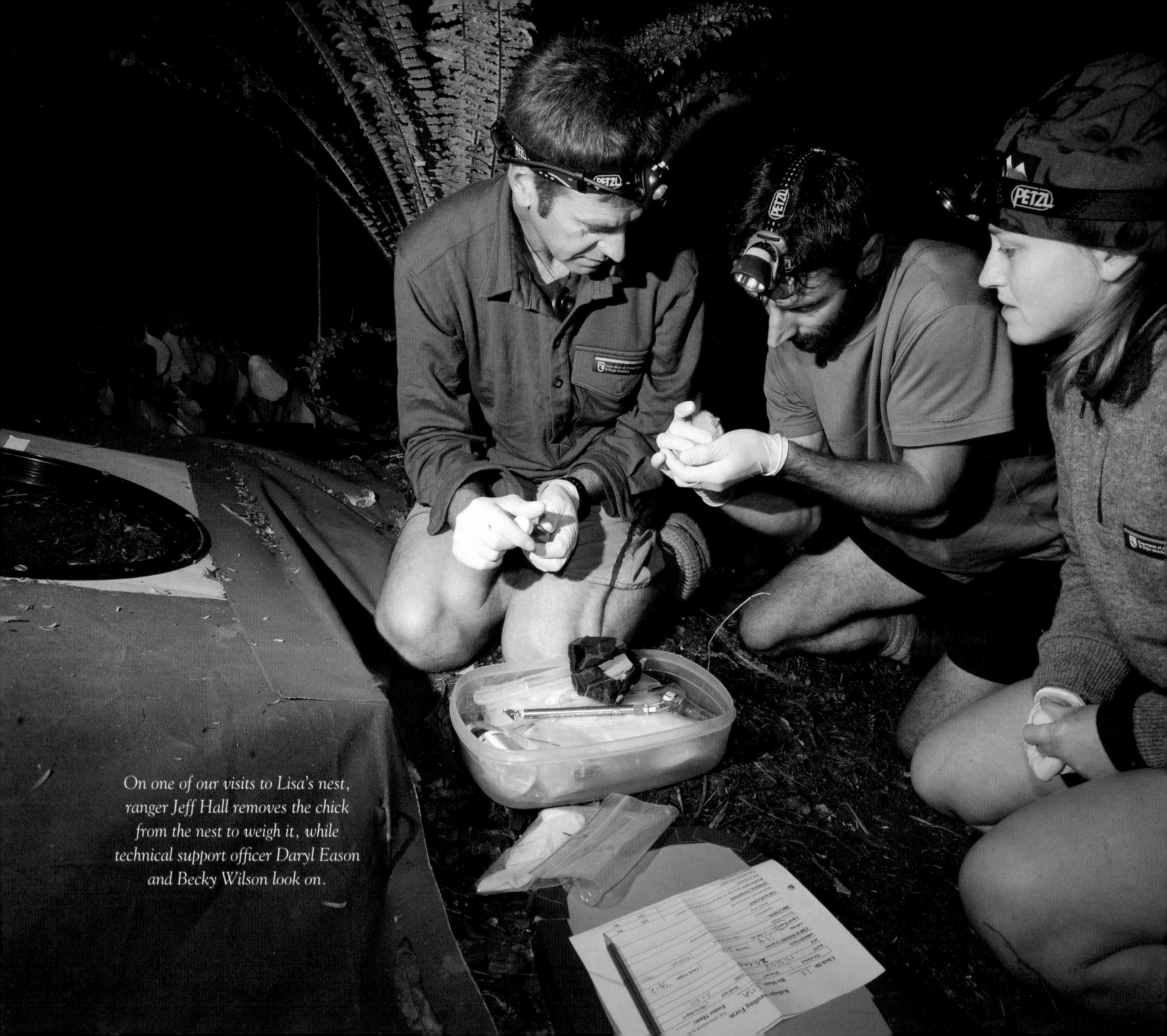

On one of our visits to Lisa's nest, ranger Jeff Hall removes the chick from the nest to weigh it, while technical support officer Daryl Eason and Becky Wilson look on.

"It doesn't seem to put them off," Catherine said.

"They're wonderfully accommodating," said Lynnie.

"Maybe they know," suggested Catherine, "that we're trying to help."

Lisa's nest is so large, a small child could lie down inside it. "Kakapo nests come in all shapes and sizes," Daryl Eason, forty-one, a kakapo technical support officer, explains. He should know; he's worked with the kakapo on Codfish for twelve years. "One kakapo, Flossie, had a nest so big you could almost walk into it!" he tells us. But other kakapo nest inside hollow logs and under grass tussocks. Though the bird can change the hole to her liking using her strong beak, mostly a female chooses a nest hole that already exists: an abandoned hole dug by a sea bird, or a cave-like hollow created when a tree falls and is uprooted. Sometimes the holes are too small for a human to reach inside.

But Lisa's nest is as convenient as it is cozy. Ranger Jeff Hall, thirty-three, removes the lid and, donning a disposable surgical glove to protect the baby against germs, reaches one hand inside to retrieve the chick. He pulls out a mound of white fluff that at first looks like a clump of crumpled Kleenex.

Two days ago, it was an egg; it doesn't quite look like a bird yet. The only sure giveaway is the chick's beak, which is slightly pink and looks too large for a baby. In Jeff's hand, the infant parrot makes a purring sound like a cell phone on vibrate. In the presence of this tiny, helpless, breathtakingly rare creature, we are overcome with awe.

"Look at it! Isn't it amazing?" says Catherine.

"It's so helpless and vulnerable," says Lynnie. "It

Jeff can't help but smile.
He's waited years to hold his first kakapo chick.

would have no chance against a predator, would it?"

But happily, this baby has a whole team of kakapo lovers to protect it.

Jeff places the chick in a tiny cotton-lined basket to weigh it with a portable scale. It's a crucial moment. If the baby isn't gaining weight, the team might decide to remove it from the nest to be reared in an incubator back at Codfish Base. But the scales bring good news: Last night, the chick had weighed 34.9 grams. Tonight, it's up to 40.5.

Gently, Jeff conducts a quick health check. The other rangers record his observations on the data sheet. Breathing: normal. Nostrils: clear. Vocalization: a little vocal when held; quiet, normal. General condition: belly, legs, plump and normal.

"Everything's looking good," Jeff reports to Daryl. Between the chick's head and chest there's a lump the size of a pea—the crop, where a bird stores food before it passes to the stomach. "It's full of good food," Jeff reports. "Lisa is being a real good mum."

"Good then," says Daryl. "Give the baby a stern talking-to, and we'll see it tomorrow!"

At 8:45 p.m., Jeff replaces the chick in the nest. Catherine covers the baby with the portable heating pad. So it can't smother the baby, the pad stands on three detachable legs that can be replaced with taller legs as the chick grows. "Any extra food, then, doesn't have to go into energy to keep warm—it can go into growing," Daryl had explained to us earlier.

Lynnie erects the telemetry antenna to listen for Lisa's signal. We stand quietly by the nest for half an hour. We hear the surf crashing on the beach, along with the squeak of bats and the clicking call of petrels, which are penguin-like sea birds. There's the occasional squawk of a kaka. Then Lynnie whispers: "The signal's strong."

"Time to back away," says Jeff.

We pack up the heated blanket and hurry back in the dark. We turn on Kakapo TV to make sure the chick is safe and comfortable till Mama returns.

Ding-dong! The nest doorbell proclaims Lisa has waddled across the infrared beam and come home. At 9:20 p.m., her black-and-white image reappears on the video screen.

"She was just waiting for us to leave to come back," says Lynnie.

"She's going back to the chick, she's feeding the chick," says Catherine. "Cool!"

"Codfish Base, Codfish Base," Lynnie relays via radio. "Lisa's back on the nest."

"Oh, that's good!" replies Becky. "You guys have a good night!"

"She's such a good girl, staying there minding her chick," Lynnie says to us. "Look, she's tucking the chick under her. Love that baby!"

"She looks so content when she's settled down with the chick for sleeping," observes Catherine.

And now, just before eleven p.m., as the three rangers head back to the hut, Nic and I and the nest-minders also settle down in our tents. We'll have just a few hours of shuteye before Lisa goes out to forage again.

The doorbell wakes us at 2:20 a.m. and again at 3:36 a.m. Each time, without complaining, the nest-minders rise, tug on their clothes, check the telemetry, and stand watch over the chick, which they gently cover with the heated blanket, until Lisa returns.

The mother parrot leaves for one last bout of feeding at 7:17 a.m. and returns at 7:56.

We're tired but happy as we hike back to the hut in the cool of the morning. We're glad for our warm hats and fleeces after the cold night in the tent. We're glad for the liquid calls of the bellbirds and the pretty black and white tui flowing around us like waterfalls of sound. And we're especially glad for Lisa and her chick—and what this first baby in several years means for the survival of her kind.

When I had left the United States and Nic had left Australia for New Zealand, there had been eighty-six kakapo on the planet. When we had started climbing the trail up to Lisa's nest last night, thanks to Lisa's chick, there were eighty-seven. Jeff had held in his hands the only kakapo chick in the universe. "I've waited two and a half years for this," Jeff had said, his smile almost big enough to wrap around his whole face. "To be holding something there's eighty-seven in the world of . . . it's really, really great."

But then we got the radio transmission from Becky:

"Lisa's nest from Codfish Base, we've got some good news. We're all proud aunts and uncles!"

An egg in the incubator—one that had belonged to Rakiura, herself born on Codfish in 2002—had hatched while we were at Lisa's nest.

"That's wonderful hatching news, Becky," answered Catherine. "That makes eighty-eight! Congratulations to us all!"

At three a.m. Lynnie and Catherine return through the dark forest from Lisa's nest, carrying the heated blanket.

The team takes a break at Sealer's Bay Resort & Spa.

CHAPTER 5

LIFE AT "SEALER'S BAY RESORT & SPA"

As the first of the still-sleepy kakapo team huddle over hot tea at the breakfast table, our cook, Carol Gardner, opens up the refrigerator to find a surprise.

"There's a penguin in the fridge," she announces.

"Really?" asks a volunteer. "What kind?"

One of the rangers peers in to identify the species.

"Fiordland crested," she answers.

"How did it get there?" asks the filmmaker, Scott.

"I don't know," Carol answers.

Now Jeff, fresh out of bed, enters the kitchen. Looking for milk for his breakfast cereal, he makes the discovery anew.

"Know anything about the penguin in the fridge?"

Life at Sealer's Bay is full of surprises. If you're going to work at the end of the earth with a flightless, night-active parrot, you'd better be ready for just about anything!

When Daryl woke up, he solved the mystery of the misplaced penguin: It had washed up dead on the beach, and he knew a researcher on the mainland who would like to study it. The penguin was in the fridge to stay fresh till the body could be sent to the lab on the next plane out.

One mystery solved. But there are plenty more to work on here—especially about the kakapo.

During mast years, trees like rimu and kahikatea (shown here) produce tiny red fruit, which help sustain kakapo through the critical period of raising their chicks.

The Fiordland crested penguin is one of the world's rarest penguins.

"The biggest mystery we have to solve," explains Daryl, "is how to have food that will make them breed." In the wild, kakapo eat many things: They chew the stems of grasses like a rabbit, the cheeks moving rapidly; they eat ferns, roots, seeds, bark, flower nectar, and berries. But during the breeding season, kakapo need something extra. They need loads of energy: The males bulk up enormously, sometimes to twice their normal size. And a female must double her energy intake to lay her one to four eggs.

Naturalists long suspected that the kakapo's rare, irregular breeding season might be linked to the fruiting of certain favorite trees. Like oaks (have you noticed how some years there are acorns everywhere, and other years few?), many trees in New Zealand produce lots of fruit some years, and other years hardly any at all. The years of plenty are called mast years. And the tree with the best mast that seems most closely tied to kakapo breeding on Codfish is the rimu.

One reason kakapo breed in autumn, not in spring, is that's when the rimu fruits ripen. (Also, the nights get longer in fall and winter, giving mother birds more time to look for food.)

But even in a good mast year, explains Daryl, "so much can go wrong." In his twelve years working with the kakapo, he's seen it all: Sometimes the birds seem in top form but don't breed. Sometimes they breed but the females don't lay eggs. Sometimes the females lay but many of the eggs are infertile. Sometimes the fertile eggs die. Or the chicks hatch but the rimu fruit falls off the trees before it's ripe. "Suddenly there's no food for the chicks, so the females spend too long off the nest looking for food and the eggs or chicks die," he says. "That's the worst of all."

What's going on? That's what the scientists and rangers are trying to figure out: What triggers the breeding season? What makes the difference between infertile eggs and fertile ones? How to ensure healthy chicks? What is the secret ingredient in rimu? Is there a way to come up with a substitute to add to the kakapo's feed? How can we help?

To try to find the answers, everything in the kakapo's world is monitored, counted, weighed, and measured. Rangers keep track of dozens of rimu trees and count all the fruits on each one. Snarks record the comings and goings of kakapo to breeding grounds and to food hoppers, and they weigh each bird. Rangers track each kakapo. Every nest is monitored by video camera 24/7 and by volunteer nest-minders every night.

There's an important team helping off the island, too. Back on the mainland, scientists on the national kakapo team invent and refine gadgets, such as the snarks and the radio telemetry backpacks, and study kakapo genetics. Others, experts in bird nutrition, are trying to find what is it about rimu that makes the kakapo breed. To build goodwill, Rio Tinto Alcan, the company that owns New Zealand Aluminum Smelters with Japan's Sumitomo Chemical Company, sponsors one-fifth of the Kakapo Recovery Program's budget; the rest comes from the New Zealand government and from donations by companies, schools, clubs, foundations, and adults and children from around the world.

Thousands of volunteers have also offered crucial help. One year, more than one hundred volunteers came from New Zealand, Canada, Germany, Japan, the United Kingdom, and the United States just between the months of January and May. They came to clear and maintain trails; to set out supplemental feed for the kakapo; to move and repair equipment; to repair the hut and other outbuildings; to clean the latrines and cook the other volunteers' food.

Some volunteers wait for years for the opportunity to help. When they are finally called, most never get to see a kakapo—but

Wendy enjoys a very special encounter. Few volunteers get to see a kakapo, let alone hold one.

Volunteer cook Carol Gardner has the most important job on the island, making sure everyone is well fed and happy.

Freezing gale-force winds and drenching rains often sweep across Codfish Island, making fieldwork treacherous. Numbed by cold and fighting off hypothermia, technical support officer Deidre Vercoe heads back to the hut, dreaming of the hot drink that waits for her.

few are disappointed. It's enough to be able to help. It's enough to know the kakapo are there.

Volunteering "is a great privilege, really," says nest-minder Valerie Fay, sixty, who works for the New Zealand government. "It's probably the coolest thing I've ever done!" says twenty-two-year-old volunteer Ruaridh ("Rory") Davies, who sells sports equipment for a living. For some, the chance to help an endangered bird survive is life-changing. Volunteer Wendy Bailey, fifty-two, used to be a computer consultant—but closed down her business once she found out, through a correspondence course, how endangered New Zealand's flightless birds had become. Now she works part-time so she can volunteer as much as possible. "It turned my world around," she said. "I'm a true Greenie now, and trying to spread the message."

For some folks, working with kakapo was natural. Technical

support officer Daryl loved birds from the time he was five, and his first job was volunteering at a bird sanctuary. But for others, it's a surprise. Ranger Becky grew up in British cities, longing for wild animals but seldom getting the chance to see them. Ranger Tristan Rawlence, twenty-two, wanted to be a vet but fainted the first time he saw a surgery. When these two rangers were kids, they didn't even know that giant, flightless night-loving parrots *existed*—much less that they would make their careers helping to save them.

Now, from many different backgrounds and several different nations, we're all in it together. We range in age from early twenties to sixty-five-year-old Carol Gardner, a great-grandmother. Making everything from roast mutton to hearty bean soup to vanilla-frosted custard squares, she's worked as a volunteer cook here on vacations for more than twenty years.

Each of us brings different skills. Each of us will do different tasks. Scott, thirty-four, is making a film. Nic and I are creating this book. The three volunteer nest-minders will monitor Cyndy's and Lisa's nests. Three other volunteers will measure, dispense, and record supplemental food for the kakapo at hoppers set out all over the island. The rangers and technical support officers will track the kakapo, download data from snarks, monitor the eggs in the incubators, man the radios—and refrigerate errant penguins.

A message board lists what everyone's doing and when they're expected back at the hut. And if there's a moment left over, there's a list of other jobs that need doing, from washing the dishes to cleaning the two latrines.

A handmade sign by the front door to our hut announces SEALER'S BAY RESORT & SPA. It's a joke, of course: the hut is cozy, but not luxurious. A coal-fired stove warms the hut kitchen, while

After staying up for most of the night in their tent, the nest-minders review the video of Lisa before getting some well-earned sleep at the hut.

a gas stove helps Carol cook our meals. A generator provides power for lights, computers, and incubators and other equipment. In the two unheated bunkrooms, mosquitoes plague us at night. There's one shower, with hot water stained brown from leaves in the creek it comes from. But with only one shower for fourteen people, most of us shower only every other day.

In the days ahead, everyone will work *really* hard—sometimes almost to exhaustion. Yet in this modest hut, together we'll find companionship warmer than a deluxe tropical vacation. We'll encounter more surprises than we'd find at the most exotic resort. But what makes "Sealer's Bay Resort & Spa" best of all is that here we have the opportunity to help save a species. Says nest-minder Catherine, "It feels so worthwhile to be here."

Rainbow at Sealer's Bay.

A Night with Sirocco

Sirocco is as playful as a kitten, peeking through ferns and trying to surprise us.

A whiskered, owl-like face peers out of the leathery curtain of ferns on the ground. His dark eyes sparkle with mischief. Sirocco is looking for his quarry—any person who passes between his territory and the latrine after dark.

He sees Nic and makes a dash, wings spread out, like a toddler running. He heads toward Nic, then darts away. Then he sees me. He zooms forward, but by the time I can make out in the dark that yes, this really is a kakapo, he dashes back into the bush.

Sirocco—an eleven-year-old male named for the hot wind that comes off the North African desert—doesn't stay still for long. He climbs into a tree fern to survey us for a moment. Then he rushes back down.

Fortunately we are prepared for what comes next: Sirocco lunges for my boots. Next he starts climbing up the back of my pant leg, pinching my calf and thigh hard with his beak and strong claws. I offer him my arm as a perch, which he eagerly accepts. Now he climbs onto my shoulder and then atop my wool hat. He's heavy! I can feel his claws dig through the hat into my scalp as his wings beat my face with the regular rhythm of windshield wipers.

What is happening? The rangers explain to each newcomer: Sirocco is in love—with every human who passes by. He was raised by humans and has an identity problem. He is not sure whether he is a parrot or not. During the breeding season, when he's looking for love, he searches for a mate among the species that raised him.

After a few days, most of us have scrapes and bruises attesting to Sirocco's confusion. Jeff split open his big toe when he was racing downhill toward the hut, trying to run past the parrot and escape his unwanted attentions. For the next few days, Jeff will have to work indoors while his injury heals. Rory could have been badly bloodied when, fresh from a cold evening swim and clad only in a towel, he was assaulted by the lovesick parrot along the path to the hut. Wendy came to Rory's rescue, allowing him time to escape by offering Sirocco her two pinky fingers to climb. But rather than stepping up to perch, the parrot took her

TOP LEFT: *During the breeding season, a male clears a special patch of undergrowth. Then he inflates like a football (this male is only half inflated) and emits haunting booming calls into the night to attract females to come and watch him dance.*

ABOVE LEFT: *A low-tech approach is used to find out if a booming bowl is in use. Deidre stands up some twigs in the bowl, which will be pulled out later that night when the male kakapo does his housekeeping.*

RIGHT: *Sy wins a feathered admirer.*

fingers in his beak and hung on, hissing.

Sirocco means no harm. The scratches and bruises are well worth the pleasure of being with him. For he is letting us in on what was once a great unknown: the mystery of kakapo courtship.

For hundreds of years, kakapo romance was a secret. Kakapo court and breed at night, and no person had ever seen it. Not until saving the kakapo became a national priority did researchers discover what was going on—and when they did, it was almost too strange to believe.

Early in the breeding season, the huge male parrots waddle out of the forest to a flat, clear area and prepare a series of "stages" for the performance to come. With beak and feet, they carefully clear all the greenery from the ground to create a series of shallow, bowl-shaped depressions connected by little paths. When they are done, the nightly performance begins. Each male will stand in one of his bowls for his big show. He gulps air, puffs out his chest like a bullfrog, heaves his lungs, bobs his head—and lets out a *boom* that sounds like a person blowing across the top of a large bottle. The boom can be heard for almost three miles, and the kakapo might repeat it twenty-four thousand times in one night!

The male might alternate bouts of booms with series of high-pitched chings. Folks have described the sound like the chime of a cash register.

Females come from miles around to listen—and to watch. The males don't just sing. They dance, too, strutting and hopping, hoping to attract a mate.

When males gather this way to show off for the females, it's called a lek. Kakapo aren't the only ones to do it; male African hammer-headed bats perform a competitive concert of honking (with a voice box half the size of the body). In the American Midwest, male prairie chickens gather much like kakapo do and boom and dance for the ladies. Even some species of fish, moths, and flies competitively court females in this fashion. But the kakapo's lek display might be the most impressive of all.

Because Sirocco is courting people, not female kakapo, he has chosen to create his booming bowls conveniently between the hut and the latrine. For us, this makes evening use of the bathroom hazardous. Even if you're snug in a sleeping bag in the bunkhouse, you can't escape Sirocco's attentions. He booms and chings much of the night. His chinging sounds like a cross between the jingling of sleigh bells and a person having an asthma attack.

When even this performance fails to attract someone to his booming bowl, Sirocco tries another idea. If he sees a light on in the hut kitchen, he will sit on the windowsill and look in. He'll run back and forth. He'll scream a gravelly *skraaarrk*—which probably means something like "Can't you see? I'm a gorgeous hunk of male kakapo! Why won't you come out to admire me?"

Sirocco looks wistfully through the hut window for human company. You can see a kakapo stuffed toy just inside the window.

Becky downloads data from a snark that has been recording kakapo activity at the booming grounds.

CHAPTER 6

TRIANGULATION AND TRAGEDY

"Last night Lisa only left the nest twice," a sleepy Catherine reports at breakfast. "Wasn't she a good girl? And this morning, she came belting back—she was only gone an hour and ten minutes. The chick was really full!" In fact, Lisa's chick has now gained so much weight that the rangers had to weigh it twice last night. "Can this be for real?" ranger Jo Ledington, twenty-three, had wondered.

But it was true: the chick had put on 11.3 grams (each gram is .035 of an ounce), and was fluffier and even cuter than the night before.

It's good news all around this morning. The chick in the incubator, though exceptionally small, is thriving. And at Cyndy's nest, an hour's hike away along a steep trail, things are looking up, too. Daryl and the rangers had worried that she was staying away too long from her eggs to forage at night. But since volunteers erected a new food hopper closer to her nest, Cyndy's feeding expeditions are getting shorter. Tonight two rangers will join nest-minder Valerie. If Cyndy stays away more than two hours, they'll rescue the eggs and bring them back to the base camp incubator. But they'd rather Cyndy raise the chicks herself, as nature intended. Now that she's found the new hopper and its supplemental food, there's reasonable hope she'll be able to do just that.

Elated with all the good news, Nic and I join ranger Becky on a brilliant blue and breezy day in a winding, five- or six-mile hike. We'll be visiting the overlapping territories of at least a dozen kakapo, making sure each bird is well. Though we probably won't see them, by "tuning in" to their channel on the

A ranger takes a telemetry reading overlooking the south coast of the island.

telemetry receiver, we'll be able to roughly locate each one.

The process is called triangulation. Why? "We're making a triangle," Becky explains as she takes out her gear from her backpack: telemetry receiver, folding antenna, compass, and notebook. From specific points marked along the trail, she'll tune in several times to each kakapo's special channel, and mark the direction the signal is coming from. Back at the hut, she'll enter each reading into a computer program. Each reading is like a line on the map of the island. Where all the lines intersect forms a shape like a triangle. "And the top of the triangle," Becky emphasizes, "is where the bird is."

How often do the rangers triangulate? "That depends on who the bird is and what we need to know," she explains. A snark automatically records each bird who passes nearby or sits on it. But the rangers personally triangulate potential breeders and nesters during the breeding season every day. This is how they located Lisa's and Cyndy's nests: The signal showed these females had returned repeatedly to the exact same spot, five days in a row—proof they had settled down to lay eggs.

The first bird we check on is Suzanne, whose territory lies along the steep trail leading to a gorgeous view of Northwest Bay. Becky comes to the first marker along the trail. An ear tag, normally used for cattle, acts as a street sign and house number here: two letters and two numbers (which we have to keep secret to protect the kakapo against possible poachers—we have to keep their individual channels secret, too). Becky tunes in to Suzanne's

LEFT:
At times you feel as if you are walking through a fairy tale.

BELOW:
Tiny tomtits sometimes perch by the trail to catch insects that we disturb.

channel and swings the antenna in a slow arc. No signal. We head on to the next marker. No signal. But when she switches to a new channel, she picks up a signal for a different kakapo, Ellie. Becky's compass reads eight degrees. She jots the number in her notebook.

Just a few dozen yards later, at the next marker, we get a signal for Suzanne—Becky's compass points to 211 degrees. "We'll probably get close to her on this track!" Becky tells us. The signal strengthens as we reach the next marker. Becky takes the reading: 200 degrees.

We're in a dense celebrity neighborhood. Kakapo territories might cover as much as fifty acres for the birds to find enough leaves, seeds, fruits, and roots to eat. But on Codfish, because of

Male kakapo produce a loud skraark *call to announce themselves to others.*

the extra food the volunteers provide, kakapo need far less land (maybe nine or ten acres) to support them. Suzanne's neighbors include two of the most famous kakapo: Hoki, a female born here on Codfish in 1992—the first kakapo ever raised in captivity to survive; and Richard Henry, the only survivor of the Fiordland kakapo rescue. He's at least seventy years old, and perhaps older than one hundred. Becky tunes into his channel and hears his signal nearby.

A bit farther down the trail, Suzanne's signal is stronger yet. "I was right," whispers Becky, careful not to wake any sleeping kakapo. "We're going to get *very close*!" She switches the receiver to override—this means the closest signal will override all others—and the sound changes from beeps to clicks. "She's within ten meters now," Becky whispers. We've stepped off the track, and the signal is strongest at 253 degrees. We look around us. Suzanne could be anywhere: in that tree, beneath those ferns, inside a hollow log. "She's so close!" Becky says. "You think, Surely I'd be able to see the kakapo—but you don't. She's somewhere within vision, I'm sure. But even this close, and even with an animal that big, you don't see them. That's the amazing thing."

We're especially eager to check on Richard Henry. A few paces down the trail leads us to his white food hopper. His feeding station is located in a grand moss-covered space ringed with large rimu trees, like a mahogany-paneled dining room hung with green velvet curtains. "And this," Becky says, leading us to a magnificent overlook, "is his balcony." The bird's view of the Southern Ocean is fringed by graceful *Dracophyllum* trees, majestic ancient rata trees, and light green muttonbird scrub.

Richard Henry's signal is strongest here. "We're in the presence of the great man himself," Becky whispers. These days, she says, the grand old parrot moves slowly; he didn't boom or mate this year. But he maintains a stately air. Becky feels other birds might defer to his senior status. He alone, of all the kakapo now living, might remember what life was like for his kind on New Zealand's mainland.

We're now near another very special place on the island: the males' booming grounds. Three males of breeding age frequent this area: Ox, who in previous years fathered three fertile eggs with Lisa; Whiskers, found on Codfish Island and named for the cat food—what he would have become had he not been rescued; and Bill, who since his rescue from Stewart Island has fathered at least three chicks. In 1989, he mated with Flossie. One of her two eggs that year hatched into Rakiura—whose first egg, which just hatched this week, made Bill a kakapo grandfather.

The flat, high grounds of the booming area host few trees, only low-growing bushes and grasses. By day, of course, the place is deserted. We try to imagine the excitement and commotion of a night during the height of breeding: the echoing booms and chings carrying for miles, the males dancing, the females waddling over eagerly to inspect each male's performance.

The booming is mostly done by now, Becky explains, though some of the males still check their bowls occasionally, almost out of habit. A super-snark—recording the comings and goings of many birds at once—tells the story. Downloading the data, Becky later will see that on March 22, for instance, Ox arrived at the bowls at 9:10 p.m.; Whiskers showed up a minute later. Ox left at 11:46; Whiskers left at 1:24. Ox returned at 12:50 a.m. and stayed for six minutes, then returned at 1:14 and left at 1:20. Six minutes later Whiskers showed up and stayed for six minutes more before he left for the night. Bill perhaps was more sensible; he spent his time feeding at his hopper.

Becky listens hard for a signal.

Tiny Entoloma *mushrooms decorate the forest floor.*

On we go, to check on the location of other kakapo. Kuihi, a six-year-old female; Jean; Rakiura . . .

It's a long, fun, tiring day. After dinner at the hut, there'll be more excitement ahead. Becky will be going to Lisa's nest, her first opportunity to weigh Lisa's little chick herself. Other rangers will be joining volunteer Valerie at Cyndy's nest. If Cyndy stays away from her eggs too long, they'll bring them home—but they hope they won't have to.

On the hike back to the hut, Nic and I are torn: Which nest should we visit? In the end, we decide on both. We'll stay by the radio with Daryl and Jeff and tune in to Nest Mission Control. That way, we won't miss a thing.

It's 8:15 p.m.: "Codfish Base from Lisa's nest," Becky radios in. "Lisa has left the nest." As a precaution, Jeff sets a timer for three hours, just in case she's out too long and they need to rescue the chick. "But she'll return," says Jeff. "She's been so regular—a good mum. She won't be gone long."

Though we can't see our friends the way they can see Lisa on a monitor, we can easily picture the scene at the nest. Catherine and Lynnie are unfolding the telemetry and checking Lisa's signal. Becky is excited as the three head out in the dark toward the cherished fluffy chick. In just a few minutes, we'll be getting the word on how much weight the baby has put on since last night. Surely not another eleven grams, but perhaps another ten . . .

At 8:25, Becky radios in.

"Lisa's nest to Codfish Base." Her voice sounds weak.

"I think," she says, "the chick's dead."

It can't be.

"Give it a few minutes to warm up," suggests Daryl.

But the problem isn't that the chick is too cold.

"I picked it up to weigh it," says Becky, "and I think . . . it's dead. It's dead!"

Silence.

"Well," says Daryl finally.

"There's nothing we can do now," adds Jeff. He is thinking of the first night he held that little chick, a moment he had awaited for two years. I remember his smile that night—almost as proud as if he were a father himself.

Minutes pass. Or seem to.

"Are you confident it's dead?" Daryl asks. We just can't believe it.

"Yes," Becky answers. She must be in shock. Surely Catherine and Lynnie are, too. All those nights they spent in the freezing dark, waking repeatedly throughout the night, just to keep the baby warm. All those hours watching its every move on the monitor. I imagine the two human mothers, standing in the dark, the little chick limp in Becky's gloved hand. I know they must be weeping. I am weeping, too.

"All right," says Daryl at last into the radio. Becky will bring the little corpse back to base camp for an autopsy. Daryl will examine the body in an effort to discover why the thriving baby suddenly died. "See you soon."

"Everything looked so promising last night," Jeff says.

"That's life with kakapo," Daryl replies softly. "Things crumble sometimes."

And because things can crumble so quickly, he now makes a decision about Cyndy's eggs.

"Cyndy's nest from Codfish Base," Daryl radios Tristan and the others. He relays the terrible news.

A feather shed by Richard Henry, the island's most senior kakapo, lies on the mossy forest floor.

"I don't think we should persevere with Cyndy," he tells the group. "There's too much risk." His reasoning is clear. Lisa was a model mother, yet her chick died. The best way to ensure that Cyndy's eggs hatch and her chicks survive is to remove them from the nest—and hatch and raise them in the incubator.

Poor Valerie! After so many rainy, windy, cold nights of watching Cyndy come and go, now she won't have the chance to see her feed and care for her chicks. Tomorrow, at both Lisa's and Cyndy's nests, the volunteers will be taking their tents down, bringing in the equipment, shutting the nest-minding operation down. They have all worked so hard to help the mother kakapo! Was all their work for nothing?

It falls to Daryl to try to say something to cheer us up.

"They'd all be dead if we didn't do anything," he reminds us.

The Two Richard Henrys

Today, every New Zealand conservationist respects Richard Henry's name. He pioneered bird conservation in New Zealand. He was the first person to prove that you could save endangered birds by moving them from dangerous homelands to safe islands—now a method used to protect birds and other animals around the world.

But for the last twenty years of Richard Henry's life, he thought he was a failure. He believed his efforts to save the birds he loved were in vain.

Born in Ireland in 1845, Richard moved with his parents to Australia when he was six. He spent his childhood outdoors, exploring the Australian bush. He moved to New Zealand in the 1870s and worked as a shepherd, taxidermist, boat builder, explorer, and guide. But his great passion was New Zealand's birds. He was always watching them, making notes, and writing articles about them for magazines and newspapers. He was worried about the birds' survival: Foreign mammals such as cats and weasels were eating many of them to extinction.

In 1891, New Zealand's leaders began to listen. To try to protect some of New Zealand's endangered birds, the government set aside craggy Resolution Island as its first sanctuary just for birds, and in 1894 made Richard its caretaker. The job came with a small salary (out of which he had to pay his one part-time assistant), a sailboat to get to and from the island, and the wood, nails, and other materials for a house he had to build himself!

The work was lonely and difficult. The weather on the island was, as he wrote, "tempestuous": it rained two hundred days one year. During his fourteen years as curator of Resolution, he and his assistant captured and transferred hundreds of kakapo and kiwi from the predator-infested mainland to Resolution Island and other safe islands in Dusky Sound. In his first six years, he had moved seven hundred kakapo and kiwi.

As he worked, he carefully studied the birds' habits. At a time when cameras were rare, he took some of the first photographs of New Zealand birds in history. He developed them in a

Richard Henry stands in front of the boat shed that he built in Fiordland.

darkroom he built himself. He was the first to document male kakapo booming—"like distant thunder," he wrote. He was the first to suggest that the erratic fruiting of certain trees might powerfully influence the timing of the kakapo's rare and unpredictable breeding seasons.

But his hopes for a predator-free sanctuary for kiwi and kakapo on Resolution Island were dashed. In 1900, tourists in a passing yacht told him they had seen a stoat on the island's beach. At first he didn't believe it. But then he saw one himself. Somehow, it had swum to the island—and there could be more. In fact, there were. Soon there were many. He tried to trap them, but failed. The kakapo of Resolution Island were all killed.

Richard Henry was devastated. He tendered his resignation as curator of the island—but his bosses refused to accept it. He stayed another eight years. In failing health, he next took a job as curator on a less remote island—Kapiti—and then retired, a heartbroken man. He died at age seventy-six in a mental hospital. Only the local postman attended his funeral.

But today, Richard Henry would be extremely proud. His efforts *did* make a difference. His observations of many different bird species still guide scientists and conservationists' work today. The method he pioneered—moving endangered birds to safe islands—is credited with saving many species from extinction, including kiwi, kakapo, and even the world's heaviest insect, the giant weta.

Richard Henry's legacy lives on. Perhaps more than anything else, he would be thrilled to know about another Richard Henry, who has also done his part to save the kakapo. The male kakapo named in the conservationist's honor is Codfish Island's most celebrated resident. He is the oldest kakapo in the world, and was discovered in Fiordland in 1975. He is the only survivor of the Fiordland population.

His is a very different heritage from the Stewart Island birds: The greens and yellows of Richard Henry's feathers are brighter. His booms sound different from the other males—like he is speaking a different dialect—and he doesn't *ching*.

Since the kakapo Richard Henry is at least seventy years old and might be more than one hundred, no one knows how much longer he might live. No one knows the life span of a kakapo. But even when this Richard Henry is gone, like the man for whom he was named, his heritage will live on. After being moved from Fiordland, he mated with Flossie, passing on his genes to three chicks.

As long as kakapo survive, their very existence will honor the spirits of the two Richard Henrys.

Richard Henry's dog, Lassie, helped him to find kakapo in the thick forest. The muzzle was to prevent Lassie from possibly hurting the birds.

Finding kakapo in the steep trackless forest is like looking for a needle in a haystack, even when you have telemetry to help.

CHAPTER 7

FLOSSIE'S WARDROBE CHANGE

Everyone seems exhausted. Some of it is sadness; some of it is from lack of sleep. In addition to their other duties, Daryl and the rangers have been taking turns waking up every two hours to carefully weigh, examine, and feed Rakiura's chick. Feeding her a special formula in the incubator will probably keep her safe from what killed Lisa's chick.

Daryl's autopsy revealed that the pointy edges of a tiny seed that Lisa had found in the wild to feed her chick had punctured the baby's stomach.

Hopefully, more eggs will be hatching soon. With all those chicks to feed, things will soon get really hectic. Before that happens, Daryl decides someone had better change the transmitter on Flossie's backpack. The transmitters are changed yearly, and hers is about to run out. Flossie is an exceptionally important kakapo: she has produced more babies than any other mother. She is Richard Henry's ex, Bill's last mate, and the grandmother of Rakiura's chick and her as-yet-unhatched egg. Only one other bird on the island—Nora—is a documented kakapo grandmother.

Flossie's wardrobe change is a delicate and challenging process. Fortunately the perfect person has arrived to make this switch. Technical support officer Deidre Vercoe, twenty-nine, has just flown in from the mainland with her husband, Darren, and eleven-month-old baby, Zadie. She's worked with kakapo for five years. One baby kakapo hatched in her hands. Another she nursed back to health for two months as he recovered from a tennis-ball-size wound. (That bird, Doc, is alive and well and living on Anchor Island.)

Deidre has been part of more than 450 kakapo captures. Sometimes she has to climb a tree, legs wrapped tightly around the trunk, to catch the bird. Once she had to spend four nights trying to catch a particular male whose transmitter had died—but she got him. So Deidre's the perfect choice to lead today's expedition to capture and re-outfit one of only two kakapo grandmothers in existence. Rangers Jo and Becky come along to help. Nic and I and Scott, the filmmaker, will document it.

"They're not like other birds," Deidre tells us as we hike along the trail to Flossie's territory. "They captivate you because each is an individual, a character. When they look at you, you see they're quite special. Each has an individual life history. Each has a long memory." To keep them safe from rats and other invaders, the kakapo have sometimes been moved multiple times, from one island to another, Deidre explains—and, as she can tell from their movements recorded by radio telemetry, the parrots always remember the details of their old territories, even years later.

"Flossie knows each of these gullies, she knows them all so well," Deidre says. Flossie has a beautiful territory. She lives along a trail lined with giant trees that look like gnarled, bearded wizards. In the forest's dim and magical light, it looks like the trees might go for a stroll at any moment. At the trail's second marker, Deidre dials up Flossie's channel and gets a clear signal. "Let's turn down this

The dense, ferny forest provides a million hiding places for a moss-green kakapo. A kakapo will often "freeze" when it hears you get close, which means you must be careful not to step on it by mistake!

way and see where it gets us," she says to the team. She points down an almost vertical slope, off trail.

Now we're bush-bashing, slipping and sliding in the light rain that has just begun. As we descend, we hang on—barely—to the trunks of saplings, the roots of big trees, and slippery black supplejack vine. When our handholds give way, we slide downhill in the mud toward a stream. Once there, the next telemetry reading reveals—oh, no!—we have to go *uphill* next. We slog through curtains of ferns that hide ankle-twisting holes, around vines that catch and twist at our boots, and over fallen logs greasy with fresh mud.

Jo takes another telemetry reading. She points and nods. Flossie might be less than ninety yards away, and hopefully is still asleep. "Flossie can be a really good runner," whispers Deidre. But Flossie might also be placid and calm. Once before, Deidre caught her easily while the kakapo stood calmly on a log. "It depends on what dreams she's having."

The three women creep off, over the hill, each carrying their telemetry. Separated by twenty feet, both turn down the volume on their receivers so as not to wake the kakapo. Each advances on tiptoe.

But—crunch!—the sound of *Blechnum* fern crushed under hiking boots gives away their footsteps. Flossie wakes up. The telemetry's soft beeps show she's sneaking off!

Jo signals Deidre, pointing with her left hand. She's got Flossie in sight. Deidre can't see the bird—she's obscured by a dense patch of ferns and a fallen tree—but Deidre knows what to do. She advances, trying to urge Flossie back toward Jo.

Now Flossie sees Deidre. That woman looks like trouble! The parrot turns and runs toward Jo—and Jo lunges and grabs the

Deidre, Becky, and Jo (from left to right) get Flossie ready for her new backpack transmitter.

Jo checks Flossie's ears.

parrot by her strong feet. Gently holding the back of her neck, Jo lowers Flossie into a black bag, where she can calm down.

Deidre, covered in cobwebs, gives the thumbs-up. Even though Flossie is wide awake now, we still speak only in whispers. We don't want to stress Flossie more than necessary.

Deidre weighs the bird in her bag on the portable scale. Because Flossie didn't breed this year, she is lighter than the breeding females, but still is in fine fettle. She weighs in at 1.77 kilograms (want to convert to pounds? Multiply by 2.2). Becky records the data.

Now Deirdre takes Flossie out of the bag. With bare hands sterilized with Medi-Wipes, she holds the parrot with quiet confidence. Flossie is surprisingly calm. She growls from time to time, but doesn't struggle or squawk. Jo, with clean hands also, parts the bird's feathers to reveal the old backpack harness, strung beneath her wings with nylon cord. It was fitted perfectly and hadn't rubbed a single feather. She snips the nylon with scissors and slides on the new one.

The three women carefully check Flossie's condition. Becky records all the information. Flossie is plump and healthy. Her eyes and ears are clear. Her feet are smooth and cream-colored, with no sores or calluses. Her crop, the organ in a bird's neck where food is stored before it passes on to the stomach, is one-quarter full. Jo snips a feather sample for study back on the mainland. Becky tests to make sure the new backpack's transmitter is working. Flossie's channel is coming in just fine.

It's time to let Flossie go. But first, Deidre presses her nose to Flossie's feathers. The scientist's eyes close in ecstasy. "She smells so good," Deidre whispers. And then she kisses Flossie atop the head. "That's from your granddaughter," she says.

The huge green grandmother kakapo rushes off, uphill, into some ferns.

"Goodbye, Flossie," calls Jo. "It was so nice to see you!"

But then, even as she's running away from us, Flossie is overcome with kakapo curiosity. Dodging behind the trunk of a tree fern, she turns and pauses. For just a moment, she peeks back at us—then hurries back up the hill.

ABOVE: *Kakapo smell sweet and earthy, like honey mixed with peat.*

RIGHT: *Ferns smother the forest floor.*

A ranger weighs out a supplementary food mix for kakapo, made of nuts, seeds, and other ingredients.

CHAPTER 8

FEEDOUT VOLLIES

Today, Nic and I get breakfast twice: once at the hut kitchen, and again at the "Chubby Budgie Bar and Grill."

That's the name the rangers have given the feed room where the kakapo's supplemental food is portioned out. Here the ingredients are assembled with the same care that a chef takes in a five-star restaurant. Though this eatery has only a handful of regular customers, they're all VIPs—very important parrots.

Supplementing the kakapo's natural food was the idea of Don Merton, a scientist who has worked on behalf of kakapo for more than three decades. He had first used food supplements to help save the echo parakeet, an endangered species from Mauritius Island in the Indian Ocean. He hoped food supplements might help the kakapo too—and they did. When rangers set out apples, almonds, walnuts, and the sweet-potato-like kumara for the kakapo, females who hadn't bred for years produced chicks.

But the foods must be chosen carefully, researchers learned. Not just any food will do, and any ingredient might have unintended consequences. Careful experimentation uncovered that females supplemented with more nuts produced more male than female chicks. The kakapo team changed the food formula, and the next breeding season they got more females than males.

The researchers further refined the recipe. This year, the feed contains more fiber and flax oil, to make it more like rimu.

Volunteer Liz Whitwell heads out on her rounds.

And this year, for the first time, every female who bred produced fertile eggs.

The current formula features, among other ingredients, macadamia nuts, almonds, and a slurry of commercial parrot food that's mixed up and then frozen to make sure it stays fresh.

The supplemental feed is "one of the most powerful tools we have to save them," explains Jeff. "But it's something we take very seriously. We need to eliminate every chance we can that we're doing something bad. Feeding them is the riskiest thing we do."

So when you enter this bar and grill, you leave your dirty boots at the door. You slip your feet into clean clogs. You touch nothing without washing your hands. And just like in the finest kitchens, everything that touches the kakapo's food is not only cleaned but disinfected, to get rid of not just dirt, but germs, too.

Each bird's feed is carefully weighed. Based on its age, size, and breeding condition, each bird gets a different amount in his or her hopper—though of course the birds don't know which hopper belongs to whom and often eat from neighboring hoppers. Today we're going out with volunteer Liz Whitwell, twenty-eight. She'll deliver the day's meal to nine birds: Kuia, Margaret Maree, Konini, Ruth, Jean, Basil, Lisa, Yasmine, and Sirocco. She packs the food, carefully labeled with each name, along with water: of course the kakapo need a beverage with their meal, and only clean water will do. With the filled hopper bins, sterilizing Medi-Wipes, water, and her own meager lunch and drink, Liz's backpack weighs forty-five pounds. Her legs and her pack are the delivery truck.

The route today is tough, muddy, and steep. But Liz is ready for it. When she's not volunteering, she works for the New Zealand Department of Conservation on another island, Little Barrier, mowing, weeding, and helping scientists prepare a sanctuary for rare species, including the kiwi and the tuatara—the only surviving member of an ancient order of reptiles that might have had three eyes. (Only two of the tuatara's eyes work; the third is sort of like our appendix—a leftover beneath the skin that you can't see.)

We leave at ten a.m. and walk to the far end of the beach, where to our surprise, we find someone is already there: a yellow-eyed penguin! Though he's only twenty inches tall, he's completely undisturbed by the three humans staring down at him. When he sees us, he doesn't even bother to stop scratching. With a pink webbed foot tipped with black toenails, he carefully scratches first one side, then the other side of his face. Then, in a dignified way befitting someone who's always wearing a tuxedo, he shuffles forward a few steps to slide headfirst into a cool, sandy burrow.

We now enter the forest. A steep hike leaves my eyes stinging with sweat and my hair plastered to my head. We pause to catch our breath. "A nice, wee grunt," says Liz. The first feeder—Kuia's—is still another twenty-minute hike away.

When we get there, we open the hinged lid on the hop-

LEFT:
Yellow-eyed penguins come ashore to nest on Codfish Island, raising their young deep in the forest.

BELOW:
The tui is a wonderful mimic, often mixing the calls of other birds into a beautiful song of its own.

per to find Kuia's food untouched. But Liz can't just leave the food there; it could spoil. So Liz exchanges one food hopper for another. She must bring any uneaten kakapo food back to the hut, where it will be carted off the island and composted on the mainland. She dumps out the water hopper, wipes it clean with Medi-Wipes, refills it with fresh water, and cleans every surface she's touched. She does it all with the graceful efficiency of a diner waitress—even though she has no waitressing experience.

The next track is just as steep and muddy as the previous one, only more narrow and overgrown. I get stuck in a tangle of supplejack vine. A fallen tree halts us briefly; we each in turn bump our packs on it as we try to duck beneath it and won't fit. We try again. Our boots are wet from crossing a stream. But finally we reach Margaret Maree's hopper. And it's a mess!

Like kids with their toys, kakapo love to play. (They had no problem learning how to open the hinged lids on the hoppers that keep the food dry.) Just about any object will do. Margaret Maree used to use her strong beak to pull her hopper out of the U-shaped bracket holding it to the ground and toss it around like a toy. The rangers dealt with that by bolting the hopper down. But just like a naughty kid, yesterday Margaret Maree played with her food. She tossed it everywhere, and even smeared it on the little platform where she's supposed to stand and get weighed while she eats.

Liz scrapes the food away with her favorite cleaning tool: a plastic trading card featuring New Zealand rugby players that came in the Weet-Bix cereal box. Today she's scraping with player Leon McDonald. (Wonder what he'd think if he knew?) She cleans up the mess, replaces the food, empties out and replenishes the water, and wipes everything down to sterilize it.

On we go. Along the miles and miles of trail, we want to look up at the beautiful tree ferns, the huge rata and rimu. But the way is treacherous—slippery, tangled, and booby-trapped with holes, the burrows of the fatty mutton birds that sustained the first settlers here. The trails seem designed to break human ankles. By early afternoon, my leg muscles start to feel as if they are on fire.

Even Nic is tired; he has all the photos he needs today. I am exhausted. So when we happen to cross paths with Jo, who's nearly completed her triangulation circuit, we're delighted when the ranger offers to lead us back to the hut while Liz visits the final three hoppers. As we head home, Nic and Jo get ahead of me as I trip over roots on my shaking legs.

I see they've stopped not far from the hut. Jo has her radio out. I race to catch up and hear what's happening.

"Jo-Jo, Jo-Jo, this is Codfish Base."

"Jo here—over."

"Did you hear the news?"

"No, I haven't."

Then, an ominous pause.

"Bill has died."

How can it be possible? We just heard his signal the other day with Becky. Wendy, on feed-out duty, had only just filled his bowl yesterday. She had found one of his sweet-scented feathers nearby. "Thank you, Bill," she had said, in case he was nearby listening, "for leaving this beautiful present for me!"

Tristan was up near the booming bowls triangulating today when he tuned in to Bill's channel. To his horror, he got the sad, distinctive "mortality" signal that sounds when a bird has not moved in a long time: a fast *beep-beep-beep,* urgent as a heart attack. But in this case, there was nothing to be done. Tristan found

Liz changes the food and drink at each feed station and then wipes everything clean.

BELOW:
Bellbirds fill the forest with beautiful ringing calls.

RIGHT:
Ferns and mosses clothe an ancient rata trunk.

Bill's body is taken by helicopter to the mainland, for autopsy by special vets.

Bill's body lying peacefully near the track, with no sign of a fight or an injury.

We're all stunned—but we realize we must hurry back to camp. It's bad enough that Bill has died. But what if he died of a contagious disease? What if there was something wrong with the food? Are the other kakapo in danger? *What should we do?*

Back at camp, Daryl and Deidre's decision is swift. They both remember the terrible day back in 2005 when several kakapo died because some of the walnuts in their food mixture had spoiled, producing a poisonous fungus called aflotoxin. Walnuts are no longer used in the food, but no one is taking any chances. The volunteers and rangers, already dog-tired after a long day, head back out to retrieve as many hoppers as possible. They'll remove all the food they just set out. They'll clean and Medi-Wipe everything. Even Jeff, with his injured toe, puts on his boots and hikes up the mountain track to help. Many of them won't be back until long after dark.

Daryl phones the mainland to send a helicopter to take Bill's body for autopsy at the Auckland Zoo's Center for Conservation Medicine. It arrives on Codfish at 7:20 p.m. There's no time to lose. We should have an answer in two or three days.

All of us left at camp walk out to watch Bill's body, packed in a blue and white picnic cooler, loaded into the helicopter, and say farewell.

"Poor old Bill," says Scott as the helicopter flies off. "At least he lived to be a grandfather."

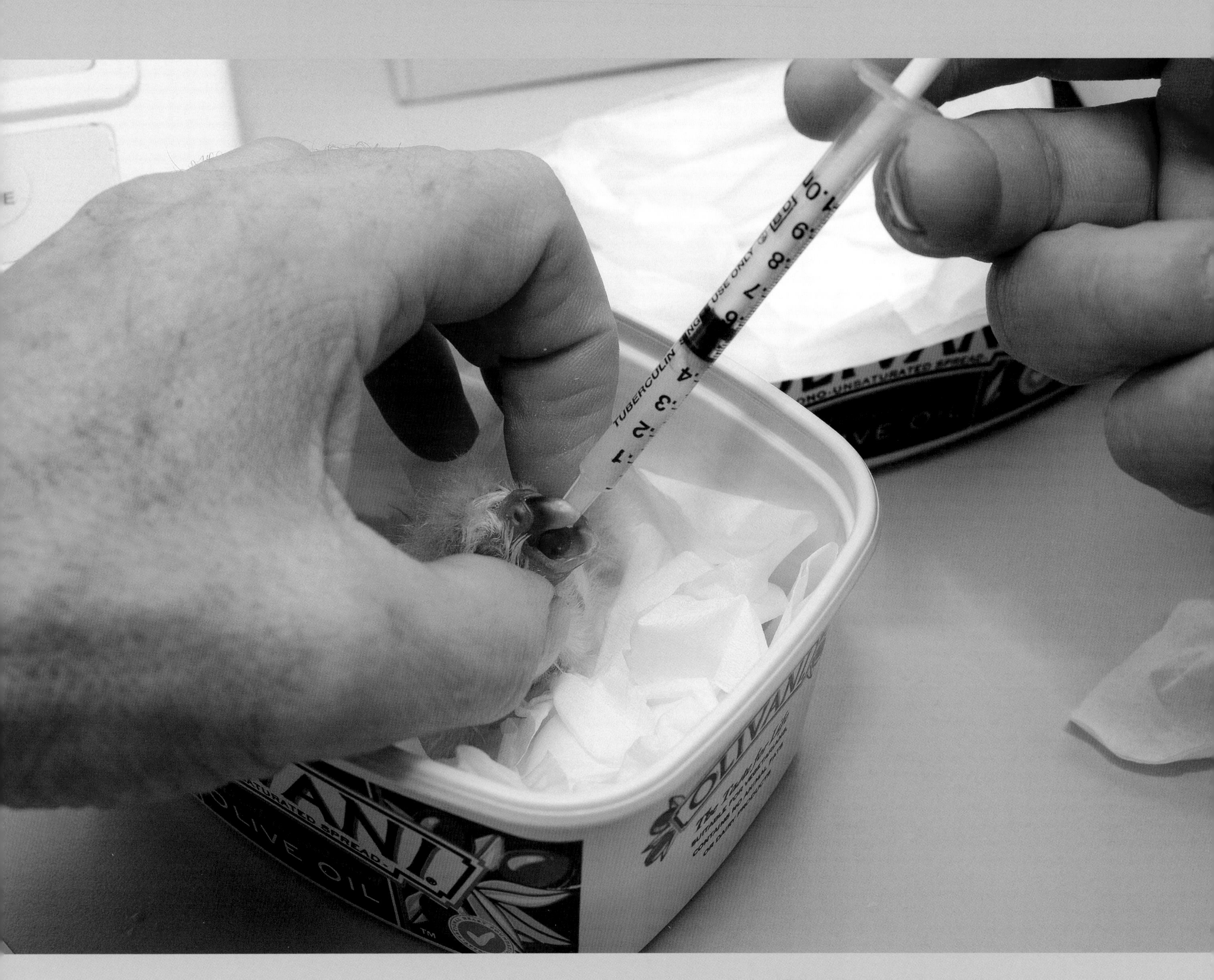

Daryl slowly feeds the young chick with special kakapo baby food.

CHAPTER 9

HATCH WATCH

The nest-minders have folded their tents. The only kakapo on nests now are the images recorded on the kakapo TV monitors. Valerie, who had watched Cyndy's nest, reviews the tape of Cyndy looking for the eggs the rangers rescued while she was foraging. Catherine and Lynnie watch the tape of Lisa's return to the nest to find her chick was gone.

She spent eleven minutes walking in circles, searching for the baby. Then she left again. When she returned, she preened her feathers absentmindedly, and according to Catherine, "looked like she was talking to herself."

Sad though we are to abandon the nests, now all our eggs, so to speak, are in one basket: actually, they're in two incubators, located in a boxy temporary building a few steps from the hut itself. The incubators, a bit bigger than microwave ovens, keep the eggs warm (about 37 degrees Centigrade—that's 99 degrees Fahrenheit). They turn each egg twice an hour automatically. But there's a lot of work for people to do, even before the eggs hatch.

Rakiura's chick, living in a third incubator, needs feeding, weighing, and checking every two hours. It's a complicated, precise process. Daryl invites Nic and me to watch.

First, Daryl carefully washes his hands before handling anything that might touch the chick. He warms up the water that will be mixed with the chick's food, and tests the temperature. It must be between 40 and 43 degrees Centigrade (about 104–109° F).

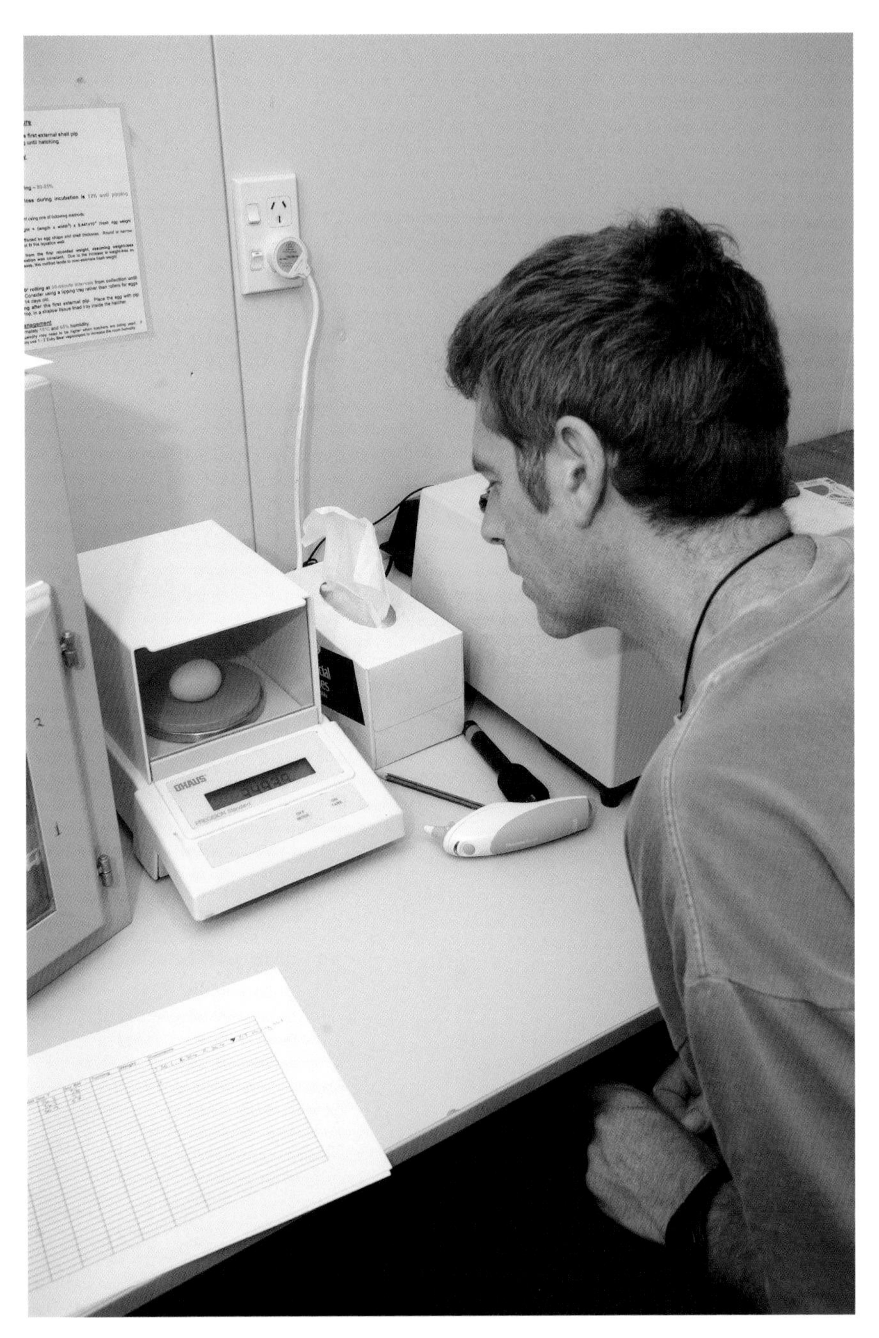

Daryl checks the weight of each egg from the incubator.

Then he mixes up breakfast: a rich slurry of Kaytee Chick Feed for baby parrots, and extra fiber. He transfers the slurry to a sterile syringe, and then reaches into the incubator for Rakiura's little chick, cradled in a tissue-lined olive oil spread tub. At three days old, it now weighs as much as a normal kakapo newborn: 24.03 grams, less than a handful of change.

The baby begs enthusiastically. Its whole body vibrates as it utters a very un-chick-like purring sound. Daryl holds its strangely large, purplish beak open with the fingers of one hand while slowly squirting feed from the syringe with the other.

"There you go," Daryl says gently to the chick. "Keep up the good work," he says as he places it back in its incubator. "We'll see about getting you some company soon."

In the two adjoining incubators, the eggs must be weighed every day. Each is checked for a heartbeat with a digital egg monitor. (Near hatching, the heart rate is around 250 beats per minute.) The temperature of each egg is taken with the sort of thermometer that takes the temperature in young children's ears, and is dutifully recorded. (It should be around 36 or 37 degrees Celsius.) It's important to check on each egg's progress, just like doctors check on a baby before it is born.

Rakiura's second egg could hatch any day now. It's the smallest kakapo egg ever recorded in the history of the project. With a special bump on its beak called an egg tooth, the baby made a tiny crack at the blunt end of the egg this morning, a process called pipping. But getting out of the egg could take hours. The chick could still be at it well into the night.

Every one and a half hours, a ranger is assigned to check

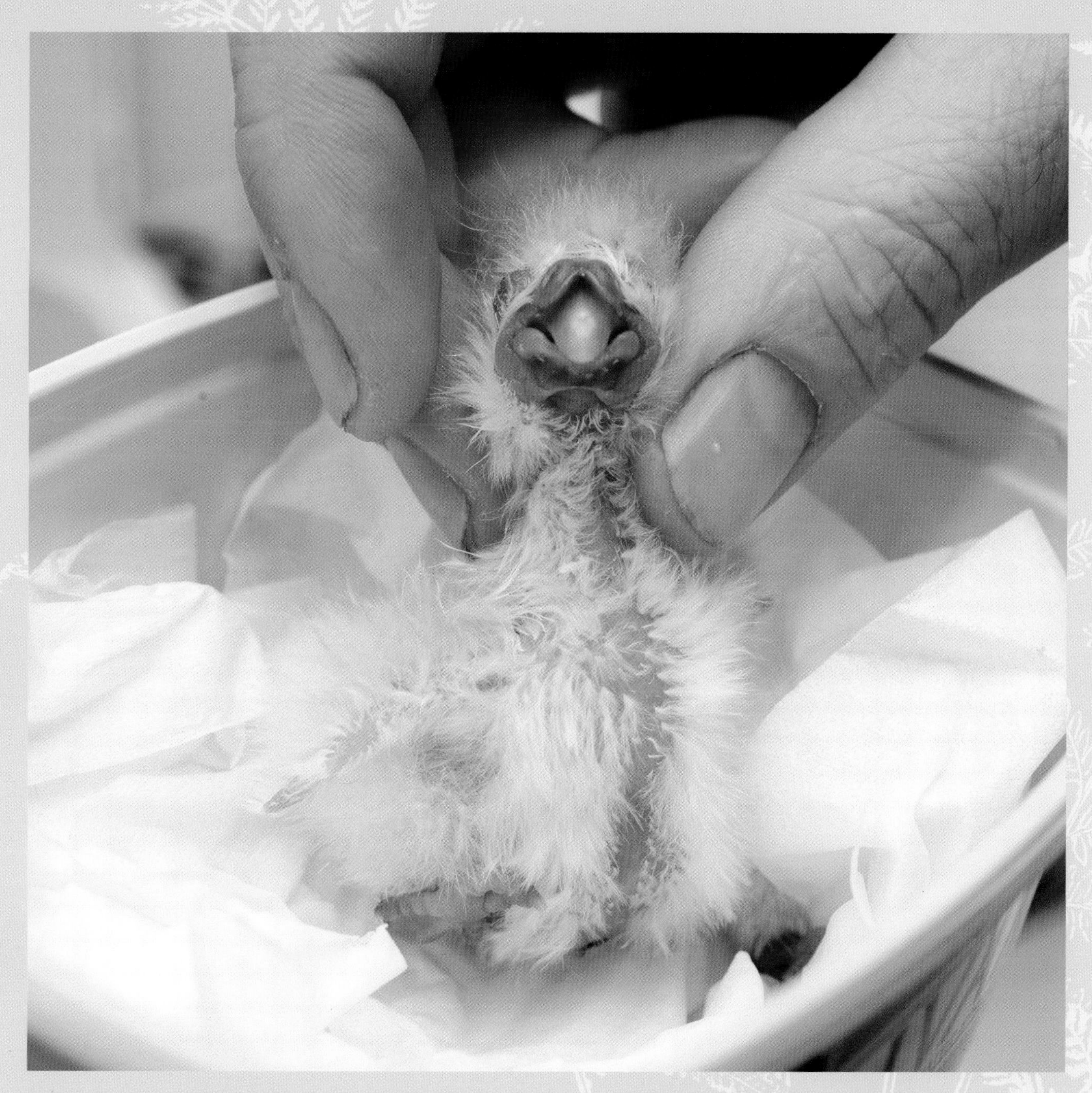

After its first feed, the chick will be returned to its temperature-controlled incubator.

the egg, in case the chick needs help. Sometimes, the membrane lining the egg can get caught on the baby and smother it. But if you intervene too soon, you can kill a hatchling. "In the transition from life in an egg to life out of an egg," Daryl explains, "a lot is going on physiologically for the chick." In the last hours before hatching, the yolk, the yellow part of the egg, gets drawn into the chick's belly; it's an important food source, in addition to the food the mother feeds it. After the yolk is drawn in, blood vessels in the egg close down, and the blood in them, too, is also drawn inside the chick's body. That's why intervening with a hatching chick is so dangerous: "Going in early can cause bleeding or can cause the baby to hatch while the yolk is still outside the body—it can cause all sorts of complications and infection, if not death," Daryl says. So until the baby is safely out of the egg, we are all anxious.

The day drags on, and still no chick. Come night, long after supper, the light stays on in the hut. Sirocco comes to investigate, and *skraarks* loudly in disapproval when people are too busy to visit with him. Rangers are posted on Hatch Watch through the night. Nic and I retire to the bunkhouse to rest and await the news.

"It's hatching!"

Just after midnight, Jeff wakes Nic, and Nic wakes me. We launch out of our bunks. We'd been sleeping with everything but our boots on.

We join Jeff, Daryl, and Becky in the incubator room. The yellow machine's window panel is covered with a blue cloth. Even though the bird's eyes don't open at hatching, the cloth might provide a calmer environment. The edge of the plastic olive oil tub is covered in blue oxygen hose so nothing sharp can touch the delicate egg—or hurt the baby who hatches from it.

We all sit on benches, chatting in low voices. We expect this might take a while. Because the egg is so small, we expect a longish struggle.

Daryl peeks behind the blue cloth. "It's out!" he cries.

A purplish wet chick kicks and wiggles beside the newly split eggshell.

"Hey, look at you!" says Jeff.

Rakiura's first chick had struggled out of the egg only to try to crawl back in it. But this one kicks away the shell with one scaly leg, ready to take on the world. "He's a strong one!" exclaims Jeff.

"Very feisty," agrees Daryl.

"Like a Ninja turtle!" says Becky.

It's now 12:25 a.m. and the baby is clearly tired from the hard work of hatching. It lies on its tummy, the skin showing bright pink beneath the wet, white down plastered against its impossibly fragile frame. It lies in a wet heap, one foot still in the half of the egg it didn't kick away—but fully arrived into this world.

The baby flips over to its other side, now totally free of both halves of the egg. With blue-gloved hands, Daryl gently lifts it to be weighed. The baby buzzes like a bumblebee and waves its stumpy wings. It may be feisty, but it's tiny: it weighs 18.83 grams. This chick weighs three grams less than its nestmate—as light a kakapo chick as has ever hatched from an incubator. Daryl also weighs everything the hatching baby has left behind: the eggshell, some blood, the membrane lining the egg and the waste excreted by the chick while it was in the shell. These total 36.05 grams—so much more than the baby itself!

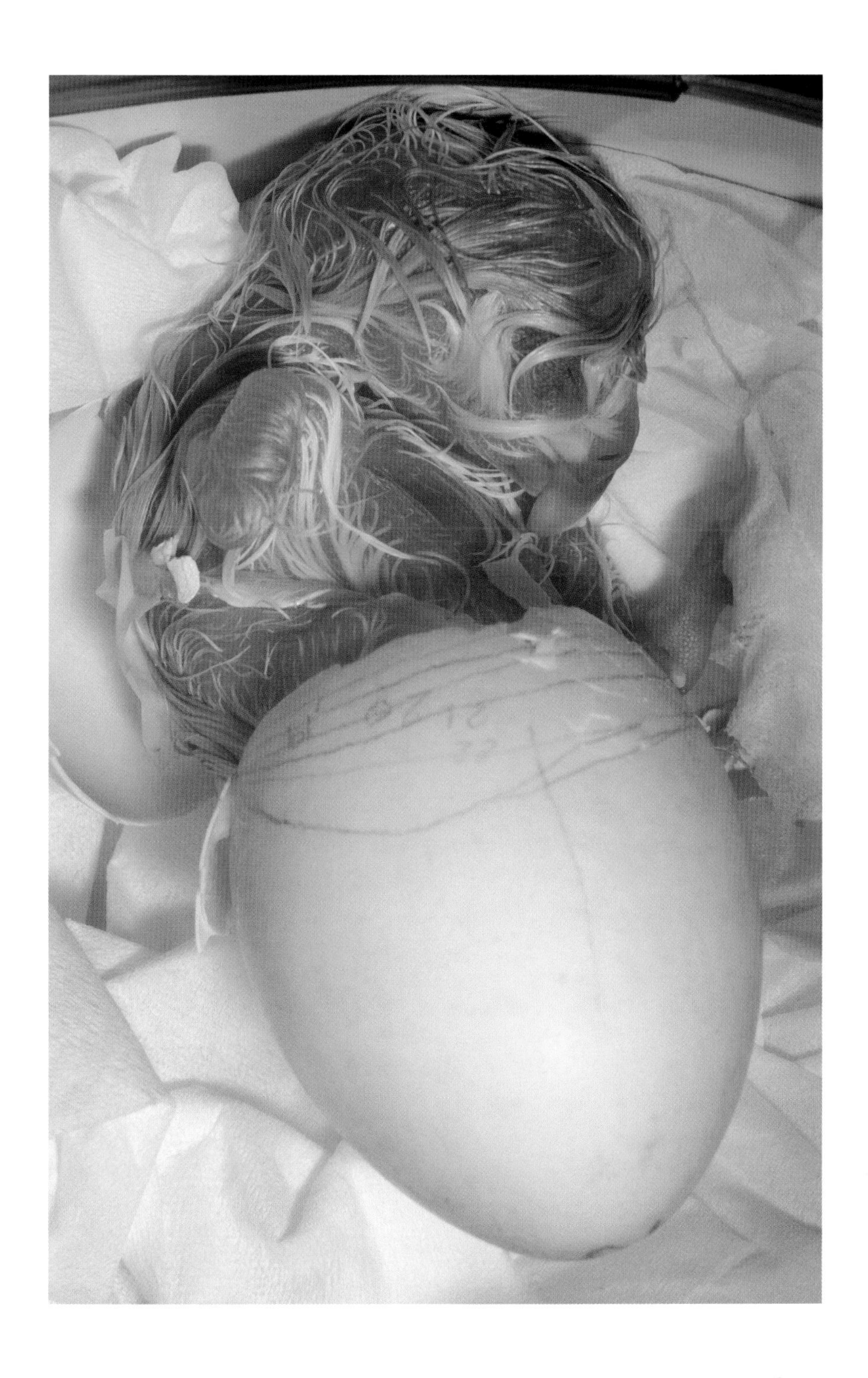

At 1:10 all the weighing and measuring is over. "Done!" proclaims Daryl. And then to the chick he says gently, "You rest for a while." He'll be up to feed it in four hours, at 4:30 a.m. Good thing Daryl practiced this sort of thing when his own baby son was born three years ago.

The rest of us are tired but elated.

"A worthy replacement for Bill," Jeff pronounces.

"Cool!" says Daryl. "We're up to eighty-seven again!"

With a wriggle and a kick, kakapo number eighty-seven makes its way into the world.

Face-to-face with Sinbad—a dazzling encounter.

Final Glimpse

Blessing at Cyndy's Lookout

We have only a few more days left on Codfish Island. Visitors are only allowed for short periods; our ten-day permit is about to expire. Nic and I choose an easy, gentle hike, hoping to take good pictures of the forest on a day when the light is soft and the weather warm. This is an unhurried day to look carefully at orchids, the bark of trees, the forest floor. It seems like a storybook setting.

Everything is green, alive, and fresh. Ferns are everywhere: tall ferns, short ferns, frilly ferns, leathery ferns, ferns that perch on treetops, ferns that climb high into the canopy, tree ferns. The ground is carpeted with lichen and soft green moss. One kind is called umbrella moss, and each plant is small enough to make a parasol perfect for a fairy.

Shortly after noon, we come to a beautiful overlook, with views of the tops of tree ferns below. Two moss-covered logs offer perfect seats for lunch. This place is called Cyndy's Lookout, as it is not far from her nest. We listen to the voices of the forest: of the bellbirds' liquid notes, the duets of the imitative tuis, the "Salt-PEA-nuts!" call of the kakas. The notes seem to fly and twirl and flip like erratic butterflies—a wild song of praise to a magical forest unlike any other on earth.

We have just finished our sandwiches when we hear rustling in the ferns.

"What is it?" I ask Nic, who has a better view of the ferns than I. "Who's there?"

We could not have been more surprised, or more honored, when a kakapo hopped out through the ferns to visit us during the daytime.

A flat, yellow whiskered face pokes out of the ferns, brown eyes curious.

"A kakapo!"

The huge parrot steps out from the ferns, pigeon-toed, a little hesitant. Later, we would learn who it is: Sinbad, a ten-year-old son of Richard Henry and Flossie. Sinbad waddles over to my backpack and gazes up at me quizzically.

I could not have been more dazzled had he been a fairy—or an angel.

But Nic and I must think fast. We snatch away the plastic refuse of our lunch so he can't chew on it. We make sure there are no crumbs he can eat. Becky had warned us never to eat near the kakapo's food hoppers, to avoid introducing unnatural or dangerous foods or germs.

Sinbad is different from Sirocco. Because Sirocco is so fond of people, he has never even tried to mate with female kakapo—and maybe never will. Sinbad was also raised by people, but has chosen a wild life. He could one day become a kakapo dad. Nic and I didn't want to do anything to change his course. The less contact Sinbad had with people, the better.

So I am careful to keep my hands away from Sinbad. But as he and I stare into each other's faces, the moment feels as sweet as a kiss.

Next Sinbad waddles over to Nic. And even though I have never heard Nic gasp for breath on any of our tiring hikes together, now I hear him breathing hard. Two conflicting desires seize him: the photographer's wish to get the shots of a lifetime of a bird so endangered, most will never see one—and the conservationist's pledge not to risk any interference that could threaten this extremely rare gem of a creature, one of fewer than ninety alive.

We stay with Sinbad only five minutes, and then move off. When we leave, our hearts are racing, our hands shake.

"I don't think we pestered the bird," I say.

"I still feel sort of guilty," says Nic.

Part of that guilt stems from just being a person in a world horribly overcrowded with humans, our pets, pests, buildings, factories, roads, and poisons. We are a species that seems to make a mess of the natural world wherever we go. Sometimes it's because we don't know enough: people didn't set out to wipe out the kakapo. Sometimes it's because we don't care enough: nation-wide efforts to save the species could have started much sooner, but people thought there were better things to do.

What a foolish mistake! "This is so much more important than what I usually do all day," volunteer Catherine had told us. She has an important government job in New Zealand's capital. But compared to saving a species, she says, her job is nothing more than "arguing over things that really don't matter.

"You come here and it's so on the brink," she told us. "This is a life-and-death struggle."

We had seen, during our days on Codfish, just how desperate that struggle is. Though kakapo had once been as common as America's buffalo, human mistakes had reduced them to such low numbers that no one could figure out how to restore nature's balance. We thought of all the years of work by so many conservationists, all the money and hours donated, that it took to bring us to this point: adding just a few more kakapo to the world population.

And here we were with one of them. How I would have loved to stay longer with Sinbad! How Nic would have loved to have taken more photos! But humans—usually without meaning to—had brought such woe to these gentle giants. We had been privileged to work hands-on with the experts who were watching nests and hand-rearing chicks. But right now, we felt, the best thing we could do for Sinbad and the future of his kind was to leave him alone—and take with us a memory we will treasure forever.

"That was a blessing," I say to Nic as we hike back toward the hut.

"You're right," Nic replies, "an incredible gift."

Sinbad heads back into the ferns.

P.S.: The Story Continues

Eighty-seven kakapo. That was the tally when Nic and I had to leave Codfish Island.

But the season was not over. Five eggs remained in the incubator. We were eager to know what happened to them, and we thought you would be too.

All five eggs hatched—including Rakiura's second egg, a second grandchild of Bill's. Tragically, her first chick died of pneumonia when it was six weeks old. But the good news was that by the end of the New Zealand autumn, the other babies brought the world population of kakapo to a new high: ninety-one birds.

And what about Bill? Veterinarians carefully examined his body to find out why he'd died, but it remains a mystery. There was no evidence of poisoned food or contagious disease. No other kakapo were affected.

This is not the end of the story, of course. The saga of the kakapo's struggle to recover from the brink of extinction continues—a struggle for survival you can check on almost every day. A web page devoted to the kakapo recovery program is updated regularly at **www.kakaporecovery.org.nz.**

Mosses and ferns cover each tree like a cloak of green feathers.

Help Save the Kakapo

Private donations from people around the world help keep the Kakapo Recovery Program running. You can help! It costs a little over $100 U.S. to do all the medical tests a single kakapo needs to stay healthy; a new incubator costs $8,000. Every little bit helps. Donations to the program are gratefully accepted at

The Kakapo Recovery Programme
P.O. Box 631
Wellington
New Zealand

(Be sure to put an airmail stamp on the envelope!)

Acknowledgments

Many people—and a number of kakapo—helped us with this book. We want to thank our colleagues in kakapo conservation in New Zealand: technical support officers Daryl Eason and Deidre Vercoe; rangers Jeff Hall, Jo Ledington, Tristan Rawlence, and Becky Wilson; volunteers Wendy Bailey, Ruaridh Davies, Carol Gardner, Valerie Fay, Lynnie Gibson, Catherine Tudhope, and Liz Whitwell; and filmmaker Scott Mouat.

We thank the Ngai Tahu, the Maori people of the southern islands of New Zealand, for their permission to visit Codfish Island (Whenua Hou). We thank National Kakapo Recovery Team leader Emma O'Neil for reading the manuscript. Ag and Phil McGinity provided us a great place to stay and wash our clothes with Trigrine before we left for Codfish Island from their Shiny Paua B and B. And we thank our wonderful editor, Kate O'Sullivan, for having the patience to wait all these years for the kakapo to nest so we could bring you this book.

Selected Bibliography

As with all the books we write in this series, most of our research is done on site, but here are some of the books we found that provided helpful background:

Balance, Alison, and Gideon Climo. **Hoki: The Story of a Kakapo.** Random House New Zealand, 1997.

Buller, Sir Walter. **A History of the Birds of New Zealand.** 1888.

Butler, David. **Quest for the Kakapo.** Heinemann Reed, 1989.

Hutching, Gerard. **Back from the Brink: The Fight to Save Our Endemic Birds.** Penguin Books New Zealand, 2004.

Jones, Jenny, with photographs by Rod Morris. **The Kakapo.** Reed Publishing, Auckland, New Zealand, 2003.

Index

Page numbers in **bold** type refer to photographs.